50 Hawaiian Treat Recipes for Home

By: Kelly Johnson

Table of Contents

- Loco Moco
- Spam Musubi
- Haupia (Coconut Pudding)
- Poke Bowl
- Huli Huli Chicken
- Malasadas
- Ahi Poke
- Poi Mochi
- Lau Lau
- Lomi Lomi Salmon
- Kalua Pig
- Shave Ice
- Portuguese Bean Soup
- Manapua
- Pipikaula (Hawaiian Beef Jerky)
- Taro Haupia Pie
- Chicken Long Rice
- Pineapple Macadamia Nut Bread
- Chocolate Haupia Pie
- Lilikoi (Passion Fruit) Cheesecake
- Coconut Shrimp
- Hawaiian Sweet Rolls
- Macadamia Nut Crusted Mahi Mahi
- Huli Huli Ribs
- Coconut Poke Cake
- Ono (Wahoo) Fish Tacos
- Punalu'u Sweet Bread
- Chicken Katsu
- Hawaiian Style Chili
- Mango Bread
- Kalbi Ribs
- Coconut Butter Mochi
- Garlic Shrimp
- Pineapple Upside-Down Cake
- Teriyaki Beef Skewers
- Banana Lumpia

- Taro Smoothie
- Hawaiian Plate Lunch
- Coconut Shrimp Curry
- Haupia Ice Cream
- Hawaiian Style Potato Salad
- Lomi Salmon Salad
- Poi Pancakes
- Ahi Tuna Burgers
- Pineapple Coconut Bars
- Ginger Chicken
- Ube (Purple Yam) Cheesecake
- Huli Huli Tofu
- Kalua Pork Nachos
- Macadamia Nut Hummus

Loco Moco

Ingredients:

- 1 cup white rice (cooked)
- 1/2 lb ground beef (or ground pork, turkey, or chicken)
- Salt and pepper to taste
- 2 eggs
- 1 cup beef or chicken broth
- 2 tablespoons soy sauce
- 1 tablespoon Worcestershire sauce
- 1 tablespoon cornstarch (optional, for thickening the gravy)
- Green onions (optional, for garnish)

Instructions:

1. **Cook the Rice:**
    - Prepare 1 cup of white rice according to package instructions. Keep warm.
2. **Form and Cook the Patties:**
    - Season the ground beef with salt and pepper.
    - Divide the seasoned ground beef into 2 portions and shape them into patties.
    - Heat a skillet over medium-high heat. Cook the patties for about 4-5 minutes per side, or until cooked through and browned. Remove from skillet and set aside.
3. **Make the Gravy:**
    - In the same skillet, add beef or chicken broth, soy sauce, and Worcestershire sauce. Bring to a simmer.
    - If you prefer a thicker gravy, mix cornstarch with a tablespoon of cold water to make a slurry. Stir the slurry into the simmering broth mixture and cook until the gravy thickens slightly, about 1-2 minutes.
4. **Fry the Eggs:**
    - In a separate non-stick skillet, fry two eggs sunny-side up or over-easy, depending on your preference.
5. **Assemble the Loco Moco:**
    - Place a serving of cooked rice on a plate.
    - Top the rice with a hamburger patty.
    - Place a fried egg on top of the patty.
    - Pour the gravy over the egg and patty.
    - Garnish with chopped green onions if desired.
6. **Serve immediately** while warm.

Enjoy your homemade Loco Moco, a delicious and comforting Hawaiian dish!

Spam Musubi

Ingredients:

- 1 can (12 oz) Spam
- 2 cups sushi rice (short-grain rice)
- 2 cups water
- 2 tablespoons rice vinegar
- 2 tablespoons sugar
- 1 teaspoon salt
- 5 sheets nori (seaweed sheets)
- Soy sauce (optional, for serving)
- Furikake (optional, for sprinkling on rice)

Instructions:

1. **Prepare the Rice:**
   - Rinse the sushi rice under cold water until the water runs clear.
   - Combine rice and water in a rice cooker or pot. Cook according to package instructions.
2. **Season the Rice:**
   - In a small bowl, mix rice vinegar, sugar, and salt until dissolved.
   - Once the rice is cooked, transfer it to a large bowl and gently fold in the vinegar mixture using a rice paddle or spatula. Let the rice cool to room temperature.
3. **Prepare the Spam:**
   - Slice the Spam lengthwise into 1/4 to 1/2 inch thick slices.
   - Heat a non-stick skillet over medium heat. Fry the Spam slices until they are golden brown and slightly crispy on each side. Remove from heat and set aside.
4. **Assemble the Spam Musubi:**
   - Lay a sheet of nori on a clean surface, shiny side down.
   - Place a Spam slice in the center of the nori sheet.
   - Using a musubi press or your hands, press a layer of rice over the Spam, compacting it slightly.
   - Fold the nori over the rice and Spam, using a little water to seal the edge of the nori. Press gently to seal.
5. **Slice and Serve:**
   - Use a sharp knife to slice the Spam Musubi into bite-sized pieces. If desired, sprinkle with furikake for extra flavor.
6. **Serve:**
   - Serve Spam Musubi as a snack or lunch item. Optionally, serve with soy sauce for dipping.

Enjoy your homemade Spam Musubi, a tasty and iconic Hawaiian treat!

Haupia (Coconut Pudding)

Ingredients:

- 1 can (13.5 oz) coconut milk (full-fat)
- 1 cup whole milk (or coconut milk for a richer flavor)
- 1/2 cup sugar
- 1/2 cup cornstarch
- 1/2 cup water
- 1 teaspoon vanilla extract (optional)

Instructions:

1. **Prepare the Coconut Mixture:**
   - In a saucepan, combine the coconut milk, whole milk (if using), and sugar over medium heat. Stir until the sugar is dissolved and the mixture is heated through, but not boiling.
2. **Mix the Cornstarch Slurry:**
   - In a small bowl, mix the cornstarch with water until dissolved, creating a slurry.
3. **Thicken the Mixture:**
   - Gradually pour the cornstarch slurry into the saucepan with the coconut milk mixture, stirring constantly to prevent lumps from forming.
4. **Cook Until Thickened:**
   - Continue to cook the mixture over medium heat, stirring constantly, until it thickens to a pudding-like consistency. This usually takes about 5-7 minutes.
5. **Add Vanilla (Optional):**
   - If using vanilla extract, stir it into the mixture once it has thickened. This adds a hint of extra flavor.
6. **Pour into Molds or Dish:**
   - Remove the saucepan from heat. Pour the Haupia mixture into a lightly greased dish or individual molds.
7. **Chill and Set:**
   - Let the Haupia cool to room temperature, then refrigerate for at least 2 hours, or until fully set.
8. **Serve:**
   - Once set, cut the Haupia into squares or shapes of your choice. Serve chilled and enjoy this creamy coconut pudding!

Haupia is a delightful treat that captures the essence of Hawaiian flavors with its rich coconut taste and smooth texture. It's perfect for any occasion where you want to bring a taste of Hawaii to your table.

Poke Bowl

Ingredients:

- 1 lb sushi-grade tuna or salmon, cubed
- 2 cups sushi rice (short-grain rice)
- 2 tablespoons soy sauce
- 1 tablespoon sesame oil
- 1 tablespoon rice vinegar
- 1 teaspoon grated fresh ginger
- 1 teaspoon honey or sugar
- 1/4 teaspoon crushed red pepper flakes (optional)
- 2 green onions, thinly sliced
- 1 avocado, sliced
- 1 cucumber, thinly sliced
- 1/2 cup edamame beans, cooked and shelled
- 1/4 cup pickled ginger (gari)
- 1/4 cup seaweed salad (optional)
- Sesame seeds, for garnish
- Nori strips, for garnish
- Sriracha mayo or spicy mayo, for drizzling (optional)

Instructions:

1. **Prepare the Rice:**
   - Rinse the sushi rice under cold water until the water runs clear. Cook the rice according to package instructions. Once cooked, let it cool slightly.
2. **Prepare the Fish:**
   - In a bowl, combine soy sauce, sesame oil, rice vinegar, grated ginger, honey or sugar, and crushed red pepper flakes (if using). Whisk until well combined.
   - Add the cubed tuna or salmon to the bowl and gently toss to coat. Let it marinate in the fridge for about 15-30 minutes.
3. **Assemble the Poke Bowl:**
   - Divide the cooked sushi rice among serving bowls.
   - Arrange marinated fish (poke) over the rice.
   - Top with sliced avocado, cucumber, edamame beans, pickled ginger, and seaweed salad (if using).
4. **Garnish and Serve:**
   - Sprinkle with sliced green onions, sesame seeds, and nori strips.
   - Drizzle with sriracha mayo or spicy mayo if desired.
5. **Enjoy:**
   - Serve immediately and enjoy your homemade Poke Bowl!

Poke Bowls are customizable, so feel free to adjust the toppings and seasonings to suit your taste preferences. It's a refreshing and healthy dish that captures the flavors of Hawaii's culinary heritage.

Huli Huli Chicken

Ingredients:

- 2 lbs boneless, skinless chicken thighs (you can also use chicken breasts)
- 1/2 cup soy sauce
- 1/2 cup pineapple juice
- 1/4 cup brown sugar
- 1/4 cup ketchup
- 2 tablespoons rice vinegar
- 1 tablespoon sesame oil
- 2 cloves garlic, minced
- 1 teaspoon fresh ginger, grated
- 1/4 teaspoon black pepper
- Pineapple slices (for grilling or serving, optional)
- Green onions, chopped (for garnish, optional)
- Sesame seeds (for garnish, optional)

Instructions:

1. **Prepare the Marinade:**
    - In a bowl, whisk together soy sauce, pineapple juice, brown sugar, ketchup, rice vinegar, sesame oil, minced garlic, grated ginger, and black pepper until the sugar is dissolved.
2. **Marinate the Chicken:**
    - Place the chicken thighs in a large resealable plastic bag or a shallow dish. Pour half of the marinade over the chicken, reserving the other half for basting later. Seal the bag or cover the dish, and refrigerate for at least 2 hours or overnight for best flavor.
3. **Grill the Chicken:**
    - Preheat your grill to medium-high heat. Oil the grill grates to prevent sticking.
    - Remove the chicken from the marinade and discard the used marinade.
    - Grill the chicken thighs for about 5-7 minutes per side, or until cooked through and nicely charred. Baste with the reserved marinade during grilling, flipping and basting several times, until the chicken is fully cooked and caramelized.
4. **Serve:**
    - Once cooked through, remove the chicken from the grill and let it rest for a few minutes.
    - Optionally, grill pineapple slices until caramelized and serve alongside the chicken.
    - Garnish with chopped green onions and sesame seeds if desired.
5. **Enjoy:**
    - Serve the Huli Huli Chicken hot with steamed rice or a fresh salad. It's a flavorful and satisfying dish that captures the essence of Hawaiian barbecue flavors.

Huli Huli Chicken is perfect for a backyard barbecue or a Hawaiian-themed dinner party. The marinade gives the chicken a sweet and tangy flavor with a hint of smokiness from grilling, making it a crowd-pleasing dish for any occasion.

Malasadas

Ingredients:

- 4 cups all-purpose flour
- 1/2 cup granulated sugar
- 1 envelope (2 1/4 teaspoons) active dry yeast
- 1 cup whole milk, warmed
- 4 large eggs
- 6 tablespoons unsalted butter, softened
- 1/2 teaspoon salt
- Vegetable oil, for frying
- Powdered sugar, for dusting

Instructions:

1. **Activate the Yeast:**
   - In a small bowl, combine the warm milk and a pinch of sugar. Sprinkle the yeast over the milk and let it sit for about 5-10 minutes until foamy.
2. **Make the Dough:**
   - In the bowl of a stand mixer fitted with the dough hook attachment, combine the flour, sugar, and salt. Mix briefly to combine.
   - Add the activated yeast mixture, eggs, and softened butter to the flour mixture. Mix on low speed until the dough comes together.
3. **Knead the Dough:**
   - Increase the mixer speed to medium and knead the dough for about 5-7 minutes, or until it becomes smooth and elastic. The dough will be sticky but should pull away from the sides of the bowl.
4. **First Rise:**
   - Transfer the dough to a lightly greased bowl, cover with plastic wrap, and let it rise in a warm place for about 1-2 hours, or until doubled in size.
5. **Shape the Malasadas:**
   - Punch down the risen dough and turn it out onto a lightly floured surface.
   - Divide the dough into golf ball-sized pieces (about 2-3 inches in diameter) and roll each piece into a smooth ball. Place the balls on a lightly floured baking sheet, leaving space between each one.
6. **Second Rise:**
   - Cover the shaped dough balls loosely with a kitchen towel and let them rise again for about 30-45 minutes, or until puffy.
7. **Fry the Malasadas:**
   - Heat vegetable oil in a large, deep pot or Dutch oven to 350°F (175°C).
   - Carefully place a few dough balls into the hot oil, frying in batches to avoid overcrowding. Fry for about 2-3 minutes per side, or until deep golden brown and cooked through.

        - Remove the fried malasadas using a slotted spoon and drain them on a paper towel-lined plate or wire rack.
8. **Finish:**
        - While still warm, roll the fried malasadas in powdered sugar until well coated.
9. **Serve:**
        - Serve the malasadas warm and enjoy them as a delicious treat!

Malasadas are best enjoyed fresh, and their soft, pillowy texture coated in powdered sugar makes them irresistible. They are a delightful indulgence that will bring a taste of Hawaii right into your kitchen!

Ahi Poke

Ingredients:

- 1 lb sushi-grade ahi tuna, cubed
- 1/4 cup soy sauce (use low sodium if preferred)
- 1 tablespoon sesame oil
- 1 tablespoon rice vinegar
- 1 teaspoon grated fresh ginger
- 1 teaspoon sriracha or chili garlic sauce (optional, for a bit of heat)
- 2 green onions, thinly sliced
- 1 teaspoon sesame seeds, for garnish
- 1 avocado, diced (optional, for serving)
- Sliced cucumber or seaweed salad (optional, for serving)
- Cooked rice or salad greens, for serving

Instructions:

1. **Prepare the Ahi Tuna:**
   - Start by ensuring your ahi tuna is fresh and sushi-grade. Cube the tuna into bite-sized pieces and place them in a mixing bowl.
2. **Make the Poke Marinade:**
   - In a small bowl, whisk together soy sauce, sesame oil, rice vinegar, grated ginger, and sriracha or chili garlic sauce (if using). Adjust seasoning to taste.
3. **Marinate the Tuna:**
   - Pour the marinade over the cubed tuna. Gently toss to coat the tuna evenly in the marinade. Cover the bowl with plastic wrap and refrigerate for at least 15-30 minutes to allow the flavors to meld.
4. **Assemble the Poke Bowl:**
   - Once marinated, remove the tuna from the refrigerator.
   - Serve the ahi poke over a bed of cooked rice or salad greens.
   - Top with sliced avocado, cucumber or seaweed salad (if using), and green onions.
   - Sprinkle sesame seeds on top for garnish.
5. **Serve and Enjoy:**
   - Serve the Ahi Poke immediately and enjoy its fresh flavors!

Ahi Poke is a refreshing and healthy dish that highlights the natural flavors of the tuna, enhanced by the savory and tangy marinade. It's perfect for a light lunch, appetizer, or even as part of a larger Hawaiian-themed meal. Adjust the ingredients and seasonings to suit your preferences for a personalized poke bowl experience at home.

Poi Mochi

Ingredients:

- 1 cup sweet rice flour (mochiko)
- 1/2 cup poi (fresh or store-bought)
- 1/2 cup granulated sugar
- 1 cup water
- 1/2 cup coconut milk (optional, for added flavor)
- 1/2 teaspoon vanilla extract (optional)

Instructions:

1. **Prepare the Poi:**
    - If using fresh poi, ensure it's smooth and well-mixed. If using store-bought poi, mix it well to remove any lumps.
2. **Make the Mochi Dough:**
    - In a large microwave-safe bowl, combine sweet rice flour, sugar, water, and coconut milk (if using). Stir until smooth and well combined.
3. **Microwave Method:**
    - Cover the bowl loosely with plastic wrap or a microwave-safe lid.
    - Microwave on high for 5 minutes. Remove from the microwave and carefully stir with a silicone spatula.
4. **Steam Method (Alternative):**
    - Alternatively, if you prefer not to use a microwave, you can steam the mochi mixture. Place the bowl over a pot of boiling water and steam for about 30-40 minutes, stirring occasionally until the mochi is cooked and translucent.
5. **Combine with Poi:**
    - Once the mochi dough is cooked and hot, add the poi to the bowl. Mix well until the poi is fully incorporated into the mochi dough. The mixture should be smooth and evenly colored.
6. **Shape and Cool:**
    - Transfer the mixture to a lightly greased 8x8 inch baking dish or a similar size pan.
    - Smooth the top with a spatula or wet hands.
    - Let the poi mochi cool at room temperature until firm and set, about 1-2 hours.
7. **Cut and Serve:**
    - Once cooled and set, cut the poi mochi into squares or rectangles using a sharp knife.
    - Serve the poi mochi at room temperature or chilled. It can be enjoyed as a snack or dessert.
8. **Storage:**
    - Store any leftover poi mochi in an airtight container at room temperature for up to 2 days, or refrigerate for longer storage. Warm slightly before serving if desired.

Poi Mochi combines the unique flavors of taro with the chewy texture of mochi, creating a delicious and distinctive Hawaiian treat. It's a wonderful way to experience traditional Hawaiian ingredients in a modern dessert form.

Lau Lau

Ingredients:

- 1 lb boneless pork shoulder or pork butt, cut into 1-inch cubes
- 16 large taro leaves (can substitute with spinach leaves if taro leaves are not available)
- Sea salt or Hawaiian salt, to taste
- 1 cup water (or enough to moisten the leaves)
- Ti leaves or foil, for wrapping (optional, but traditional)
- Steamer or large pot with steaming rack

Instructions:

1. **Prepare the Taro Leaves:**
   - Rinse the taro leaves thoroughly under cold water to remove any dirt or residue. Trim off the tough stems and set aside.
2. **Prepare the Pork:**
   - Season the pork cubes with sea salt or Hawaiian salt to taste.
3. **Wrap the Lau Lau:**
   - Lay two taro leaves overlapping each other to form a cross shape.
   - Place a portion of seasoned pork in the center of the leaves.
   - Wrap the leaves around the pork to form a tight bundle. Fold the leaves over the pork and secure tightly.
4. **Wrap with Ti Leaves or Foil (optional):**
   - If using ti leaves, wrap each bundle in a ti leaf and tie securely with kitchen twine. If ti leaves are not available, wrap tightly in aluminum foil.
5. **Steam the Lau Lau:**
   - Arrange the wrapped Lau Lau bundles in a steamer basket or a large pot with a steaming rack.
   - Add about 1 cup of water to the bottom of the steamer or pot.
   - Cover and steam over medium-high heat for 3-4 hours, or until the pork is tender and cooked through. Check the water level occasionally and add more water if necessary to prevent drying out.
6. **Serve:**
   - Carefully unwrap the Lau Lau bundles.
   - Serve the Lau Lau hot, either as a main dish or as part of a Hawaiian feast (luau), traditionally accompanied by poi, rice, and other Hawaiian side dishes.

Lau Lau is a flavorful and tender dish that showcases the natural sweetness of taro leaves and the savory pork filling. It's a staple in Hawaiian cuisine and a delicious way to experience authentic Hawaiian flavors at home.

Lomi Lomi Salmon

Ingredients:

- 1/2 lb salted salmon (or substitute with smoked salmon)
- 4 ripe tomatoes, seeded and diced
- 1 small sweet onion, finely chopped
- 2 green onions, thinly sliced
- 1/2 teaspoon red pepper flakes (optional, for a bit of heat)
- 1/2 cup crushed ice (optional, for texture)
- Freshly ground black pepper, to taste

Instructions:

1. **Prepare the Salted Salmon:**
   - If using salted salmon, rinse it under cold water to remove excess salt. Remove any bones and skin, then dice the salmon into small pieces. Alternatively, if using smoked salmon, simply dice it into small pieces.
2. **Combine Ingredients:**
   - In a large mixing bowl, combine the diced salmon, diced tomatoes, chopped sweet onion, and sliced green onions.
   - Add red pepper flakes if using, and season with freshly ground black pepper to taste.
3. **Mix Well:**
   - Gently toss all the ingredients together until well combined. The mixture should be slightly juicy from the tomatoes.
4. **Chill (Optional):**
   - For best flavor, cover the bowl and let the Lomi Lomi Salmon chill in the refrigerator for at least 30 minutes to allow the flavors to meld together. The crushed ice can be added to help keep the dish cool and give it a refreshing texture.
5. **Serve:**
   - Serve the Lomi Lomi Salmon chilled as a side dish or appetizer. It pairs well with poi, rice, or as part of a larger Hawaiian meal.

Lomi Lomi Salmon is a refreshing and flavorful dish that showcases the influence of both Hawaiian and Polynesian culinary traditions. It's perfect for sharing at gatherings or as a tasty addition to a Hawaiian-themed meal. Adjust the ingredients and seasonings according to your taste preferences for a personalized touch.

Kalua Pig

Ingredients:

- 4-5 lbs pork shoulder or pork butt, bone-in or boneless
- 1 tablespoon Hawaiian sea salt or coarse sea salt (adjust to taste)
- 1 tablespoon liquid smoke (optional, for smoky flavor)
- 1-2 tablespoons water (if using a slow cooker)
- Ti leaves or banana leaves (optional, for wrapping)
- Aluminum foil (if not using leaves)

Instructions:

1. **Prepare the Pork:**
    - If using ti leaves or banana leaves, line the bottom of a slow cooker or roasting pan with them. If not, use aluminum foil to line the cooking vessel.
2. **Season the Pork:**
    - Rub the pork shoulder all over with Hawaiian sea salt or coarse sea salt. Use your hands to massage the salt into the meat. If using liquid smoke, drizzle it over the pork and rub it in.
3. **Cooking Method 1: Slow Cooker**
    - Place the seasoned pork shoulder in the slow cooker. Add 1-2 tablespoons of water to create steam.
    - Cook on low heat for 8-10 hours, or until the pork is tender and easily pulls apart with a fork.
4. **Cooking Method 2: Oven**
    - Preheat your oven to 325°F (160°C).
    - Place the seasoned pork shoulder in a roasting pan. Cover tightly with aluminum foil.
    - Roast in the oven for 4-5 hours, or until the pork is tender and easily pulls apart with a fork.
5. **Shred the Pork:**
    - Once cooked, remove the pork from the slow cooker or oven. Use two forks to shred the meat into small pieces. Discard any bones and excess fat.
6. **Serve:**
    - Serve the Kalua Pig hot, traditionally with steamed white rice and macaroni salad as part of a Hawaiian plate lunch.
    - Optionally, drizzle some of the cooking juices over the shredded pork for added flavor.

Kalua Pig is a flavorful and tender dish with a smoky taste that's characteristic of traditional Hawaiian cuisine. It's perfect for gatherings, luaus, or any occasion where you want to enjoy a taste of Hawaii at home. Adjust the seasoning and cooking time according to your preferences and equipment used.

Shave Ice

Ingredients and Equipment:

- Ice cubes or crushed ice
- Shave Ice machine or blender (if using a blender, you'll need to blend ice until very fine)
- Flavored syrups (such as strawberry, cherry, blue raspberry, pineapple, coconut, etc.)
- Sweetened condensed milk (optional, for a "snow cap" topping)
- Additional toppings (such as mochi balls, fruit slices, or ice cream)

Instructions:

1. **Prepare the Ice:**
   - If using an ice shaver machine, follow the manufacturer's instructions to shave the ice into a fine, fluffy texture. If using a blender, pulse ice cubes until finely crushed.
2. **Fill the Shave Ice Cone or Bowl:**
   - Pack the shaved ice into a cone-shaped paper cup or a bowl.
3. **Add Flavored Syrups:**
   - Drizzle your choice of flavored syrups generously over the shaved ice. Traditional Hawaiian flavors include strawberry, cherry, blue raspberry, pineapple, and coconut. You can mix and match flavors for a more colorful and flavorful experience.
4. **Optional Snow Cap:**
   - For a traditional Hawaiian touch, drizzle sweetened condensed milk over the top of the flavored syrups. This creates a creamy "snow cap" effect and adds sweetness.
5. **Add Additional Toppings (Optional):**
   - Sprinkle additional toppings like mochi balls, fruit slices (such as mango or lychee), or even a scoop of ice cream on top of the shave ice for extra indulgence.
6. **Serve and Enjoy:**
   - Serve immediately and enjoy your homemade Shave Ice with a spoon and straw. Mix the flavors and toppings as you eat for a delightful and refreshing treat.

Shave Ice is a fun and customizable dessert that captures the essence of Hawaiian tropical flavors. It's perfect for cooling down on a hot day or bringing a taste of the islands to your home. Experiment with different syrups and toppings to create your own unique combinations!

Portuguese Bean Soup

Ingredients:

- 1 lb Portuguese sausage (linguiça or chorizo), sliced into rounds
- 1 onion, chopped
- 3 cloves garlic, minced
- 2 carrots, peeled and diced
- 2 potatoes, peeled and diced
- 1 celery stalk, chopped
- 1 can (15 oz) kidney beans, drained and rinsed (or use cooked dried beans)
- 1 can (15 oz) diced tomatoes
- 6 cups chicken or vegetable broth
- 1 cup elbow macaroni or small pasta (optional)
- Salt and pepper, to taste
- 1 bay leaf
- 1 tablespoon olive oil
- Chopped parsley, for garnish (optional)

Instructions:

1. **Sauté the Sausage and Vegetables:**
   - Heat olive oil in a large pot over medium heat. Add the sliced Portuguese sausage and cook until browned, about 5-7 minutes.
   - Add chopped onion, garlic, carrots, celery, and potatoes to the pot. Sauté for another 5 minutes, stirring occasionally, until vegetables begin to soften.
2. **Add Beans, Tomatoes, and Broth:**
   - Add kidney beans, diced tomatoes (with juices), and bay leaf to the pot. Stir to combine.
   - Pour in chicken or vegetable broth. Bring the mixture to a boil.
3. **Simmer:**
   - Reduce heat to low and let the soup simmer, uncovered, for about 30 minutes, or until vegetables are tender and flavors have melded together. If adding pasta, add it during the last 10-12 minutes of cooking and simmer until pasta is al dente.
4. **Season to Taste:**
   - Season the soup with salt and pepper to taste. Adjust seasoning as needed.
5. **Serve:**
   - Ladle the Portuguese Bean Soup into bowls. Garnish with chopped parsley if desired.
   - Serve hot and enjoy with crusty bread or cornbread.

Portuguese Bean Soup is comforting, filling, and packed with robust flavors from the sausage and vegetables. It's a versatile dish that can be customized with different types of beans, vegetables, and even spices to suit your taste preferences. Enjoy this hearty soup as a satisfying meal any time of year!

Manapua

Ingredients for the Dough:

- 3 cups all-purpose flour
- 1 tablespoon sugar
- 1 teaspoon salt
- 1 tablespoon baking powder
- 1 tablespoon vegetable oil
- 1 cup warm water

Ingredients for the Filling:

- 1 lb char siu (Chinese BBQ pork), diced (can also use chicken, beef, or vegetarian fillings)
- 2 tablespoons hoisin sauce
- 1 tablespoon soy sauce
- 1 tablespoon oyster sauce
- 1 tablespoon cornstarch
- 1/4 cup water
- 2 green onions, finely chopped
- 1 tablespoon vegetable oil

Instructions:

1. **Prepare the Dough:**
    - In a large mixing bowl, combine flour, sugar, salt, and baking powder. Mix well.
    - Add vegetable oil and warm water gradually, mixing until a dough forms.
    - Knead the dough on a floured surface for about 5-7 minutes until smooth and elastic.
    - Place the dough in a lightly oiled bowl, cover with a damp cloth, and let it rest for 1 hour.
2. **Prepare the Filling:**
    - In a small bowl, mix together hoisin sauce, soy sauce, and oyster sauce.
    - In another bowl, dissolve cornstarch in water to create a slurry.
    - Heat vegetable oil in a pan over medium heat. Add diced char siu and green onions, sauté for a few minutes until heated through.
    - Stir in the sauce mixture and cornstarch slurry. Cook until the sauce thickens and coats the filling. Remove from heat and let it cool.
3. **Assemble the Manapua:**
    - Divide the dough into 12 equal portions. Roll each portion into a ball.
    - Flatten each dough ball into a circle about 4-5 inches in diameter, leaving the center thicker than the edges.
    - Place a spoonful of filling in the center of each dough circle.

- Gather the edges of the dough circle and pinch together to seal, forming a bun shape. Twist and seal the top.
- Place each filled bun on a square of parchment paper.

4. **Steam the Manapua:**
   - Arrange the filled buns in a steamer basket, leaving space between them to expand.
   - Steam the Manapua over boiling water for 15-20 minutes, or until the dough is cooked through and fluffy.

5. **Serve:**
   - Remove the Manapua from the steamer and let them cool slightly before serving.
   - Enjoy your homemade Manapua warm as a delicious snack or meal!

Manapua is a comforting and savory treat with a soft, fluffy dough and flavorful filling. It's a popular dish in Hawaii and can be enjoyed as a snack, appetizer, or even a meal on the go. Adjust the filling ingredients to your preference for a personalized twist on this classic Hawaiian-Chinese snack.

Pipikaula (Hawaiian Beef Jerky)

Ingredients:

- 2 lbs beef (such as top round or flank steak), thinly sliced against the grain into strips
- 1 cup soy sauce
- 1/2 cup brown sugar
- 1/4 cup water
- 4 cloves garlic, minced
- 1 teaspoon ground black pepper
- 1 teaspoon onion powder
- 1/2 teaspoon garlic powder
- 1/2 teaspoon smoked paprika (optional, for smoky flavor)

Instructions:

1. **Prepare the Marinade:**
   - In a mixing bowl, combine soy sauce, brown sugar, water, minced garlic, black pepper, onion powder, garlic powder, and smoked paprika (if using). Mix well until the sugar is dissolved.
2. **Marinate the Beef:**
   - Place the thinly sliced beef strips into a large resealable plastic bag or a shallow dish.
   - Pour the marinade over the beef, ensuring all pieces are coated evenly.
   - Seal the bag or cover the dish and refrigerate for at least 4 hours, or ideally overnight, to allow the flavors to penetrate the beef.
3. **Prepare for Drying:**
   - Preheat your oven to 175°F (80°C), or the lowest setting possible.
4. **Dry the Beef:**
   - Remove the marinated beef from the refrigerator and drain off excess marinade.
   - Arrange the beef strips on wire racks placed over baking sheets or directly on oven racks, making sure they are not touching each other.
5. **Slow Bake:**
   - Place the beef in the preheated oven and bake for about 4-6 hours, or until the jerky is dried and firm but still slightly pliable. Rotate the racks halfway through baking for even drying.
6. **Cool and Store:**
   - Once dried to your desired consistency, remove the jerky from the oven and let it cool completely on the racks.
   - Pat off any excess oil with paper towels.
   - Store Pipikaula in an airtight container or zip-top bags at room temperature for up to 2 weeks. For longer storage, refrigerate or freeze.
7. **Serve and Enjoy:**

- Enjoy Pipikaula as a snack on its own, or pair it with rice, poi, or use it in dishes like salads or sandwiches for added flavor and protein.

Pipikaula is a delicious and portable snack that highlights the flavors of Hawaii. Adjust the seasonings and drying time to achieve the texture and taste that you prefer. Homemade Pipikaula is a fantastic way to experience traditional Hawaiian cuisine at home.

Taro Haupia Pie

Ingredients:

For the Taro Layer:

- 1 9-inch pre-baked pie crust (store-bought or homemade)
- 1 lb taro root, peeled and diced
- 1 can (14 oz) coconut milk
- 1/2 cup granulated sugar
- 1/4 teaspoon salt
- Purple food coloring (optional)

For the Haupia Layer:

- 1 can (14 oz) coconut milk
- 1/2 cup granulated sugar
- 1/2 cup cornstarch
- 1/4 teaspoon salt
- 1 cup water

Instructions:

1. **Prepare the Taro Layer:**
   - In a medium saucepan, combine diced taro, coconut milk, sugar, and salt.
   - Bring to a boil over medium-high heat, then reduce the heat to low.
   - Simmer for about 20-25 minutes, or until the taro is very tender and easily mashed with a fork.
   - Remove from heat and mash the taro mixture until smooth. You can use a potato masher or blend it with an immersion blender for a smoother texture.
   - If desired, add a few drops of purple food coloring to achieve a deeper purple color (optional).
   - Pour the taro mixture into the pre-baked pie crust and spread it evenly. Allow it to cool and set while you prepare the haupia layer.
2. **Prepare the Haupia Layer:**
   - In a medium saucepan, combine coconut milk, sugar, cornstarch, and salt.
   - Stir in water until smooth and well combined.
   - Cook over medium heat, stirring constantly, until the mixture thickens and comes to a boil. This will take about 5-7 minutes.
   - Remove from heat and continue stirring for another minute.
   - Pour the haupia mixture over the cooled taro layer in the pie crust. Spread it evenly with a spatula.
3. **Chill and Serve:**
   - Allow the Taro Haupia Pie to cool at room temperature for about 30 minutes.
   - Transfer the pie to the refrigerator and chill for at least 2-3 hours, or until set.

4. **Serve:**
    - Once set, slice the Taro Haupia Pie into wedges and serve chilled.
    - Enjoy the creamy coconut haupia layer complemented by the smooth and slightly sweet taro layer, all in a delicious pie crust!

Taro Haupia Pie is a refreshing and unique dessert that showcases the flavors of Hawaii. It's perfect for special occasions or whenever you're craving a taste of the islands. Adjust the sweetness or taro flavor to your liking for a personalized treat that will impress family and friends.

Chicken Long Rice

Ingredients:

- 1 lb boneless, skinless chicken thighs or breasts, thinly sliced
- 6 cups chicken broth
- 4 oz bean thread noodles (also known as glass noodles or cellophane noodles)
- 2-inch piece ginger, peeled and thinly sliced
- 4 green onions, chopped (separate white and green parts)
- 2 cloves garlic, minced
- 2 tablespoons soy sauce
- 1 tablespoon oyster sauce
- 1 tablespoon sesame oil
- Salt and pepper, to taste
- Optional: 1 teaspoon chili garlic sauce or Sriracha for heat
- Fresh cilantro or parsley, chopped (for garnish)

Instructions:

1. **Prepare the Noodles:**
    - Place the bean thread noodles in a large bowl and cover with boiling water. Let them soak for about 5-7 minutes until softened.
    - Drain the noodles and set them aside.
2. **Cook the Chicken:**
    - In a large pot or Dutch oven, heat a tablespoon of sesame oil over medium-high heat.
    - Add the sliced chicken and cook until browned and cooked through, about 5-7 minutes.
    - Remove the chicken from the pot and set it aside.
3. **Prepare the Broth:**
    - In the same pot, add the ginger slices, white parts of the green onions, and minced garlic. Sauté for 1-2 minutes until fragrant.
    - Pour in the chicken broth, soy sauce, oyster sauce, and optional chili garlic sauce or Sriracha. Bring to a boil.
4. **Simmer:**
    - Reduce the heat to medium-low and let the broth simmer for about 10 minutes to allow the flavors to meld together.
    - Add the cooked chicken back into the pot.
5. **Add Noodles and Finish:**
    - Stir in the soaked and drained bean thread noodles. Cook for another 2-3 minutes until the noodles are heated through and tender.
    - Season with salt and pepper to taste.
6. **Serve:**

- Ladle Chicken Long Rice into bowls. Garnish with chopped green onions (green parts) and fresh cilantro or parsley.
- Serve hot and enjoy this comforting Hawaiian dish!

Chicken Long Rice is a light yet satisfying dish that's perfect for any occasion. It's known for its delicate flavors and soothing broth, making it a favorite among locals and visitors alike in Hawaii. Adjust the seasonings and spice level to suit your taste preferences for a personalized touch.

Pineapple Macadamia Nut Bread

Ingredients:

- 1 cup crushed pineapple (drained)
- 1/2 cup macadamia nuts, chopped (plus extra for topping)
- 1/2 cup unsalted butter, melted
- 1 cup granulated sugar
- 2 large eggs
- 1 teaspoon vanilla extract
- 1 1/2 cups all-purpose flour
- 1 teaspoon baking powder
- 1/2 teaspoon baking soda
- 1/2 teaspoon salt
- Optional: 1/2 teaspoon ground cinnamon
- Optional: Powdered sugar (for dusting)

Instructions:

1. **Preheat and Prepare:**
    - Preheat your oven to 350°F (175°C). Grease and flour a 9x5-inch loaf pan or line it with parchment paper for easy removal.
2. **Mix Wet Ingredients:**
    - In a large mixing bowl, combine melted butter and granulated sugar. Mix until well combined.
    - Add eggs one at a time, mixing well after each addition.
    - Stir in vanilla extract and crushed pineapple (make sure to drain excess juice before adding).
3. **Combine Dry Ingredients:**
    - In a separate bowl, whisk together flour, baking powder, baking soda, salt, and ground cinnamon (if using).
4. **Combine Wet and Dry Ingredients:**
    - Gradually add the dry ingredients to the wet ingredients, stirring until just combined. Do not overmix.
    - Gently fold in chopped macadamia nuts.
5. **Bake:**
    - Pour the batter into the prepared loaf pan, spreading it evenly.
    - Sprinkle extra chopped macadamia nuts on top if desired.
6. **Bake:**
    - Bake in the preheated oven for 50-60 minutes, or until a toothpick inserted into the center comes out clean.
7. **Cool:**
    - Allow the bread to cool in the pan for 10-15 minutes, then remove it from the pan and transfer it to a wire rack to cool completely.

8. **Serve:**
    - Once cooled, slice the Pineapple Macadamia Nut Bread and serve. Optionally, dust with powdered sugar before serving for a decorative touch.

Enjoy this Pineapple Macadamia Nut Bread as a delightful treat for breakfast, brunch, or any time you crave a taste of the tropics. The combination of sweet pineapple and crunchy macadamia nuts makes it a favorite among Hawaiian-inspired baked goods.

Chocolate Haupia Pie

Ingredients:

For the Pie Crust:

- 1 1/2 cups chocolate cookie crumbs (about 20 chocolate sandwich cookies)
- 6 tablespoons unsalted butter, melted

For the Chocolate Layer:

- 1 cup semi-sweet chocolate chips
- 1/2 cup heavy cream

For the Haupia Layer:

- 1 can (14 oz) coconut milk
- 1 cup whole milk
- 1/2 cup granulated sugar
- 1/2 cup cornstarch
- 1/4 teaspoon salt
- 1 teaspoon vanilla extract

Instructions:

1. **Prepare the Pie Crust:**
    - Crush the chocolate sandwich cookies in a food processor until fine crumbs form. Alternatively, place them in a sealed plastic bag and crush with a rolling pin.
    - In a mixing bowl, combine the cookie crumbs with melted butter until evenly moistened.
    - Press the mixture firmly into the bottom and up the sides of a 9-inch pie dish to form the crust. Use the back of a spoon or a measuring cup to compact the crust.
    - Chill the crust in the refrigerator while you prepare the filling.
2. **Make the Chocolate Layer:**
    - In a microwave-safe bowl or small saucepan, heat the heavy cream until it just begins to boil.
    - Pour the hot cream over the semi-sweet chocolate chips and let it sit for 1-2 minutes.
    - Stir the chocolate and cream together until smooth and glossy.
    - Pour the chocolate mixture into the prepared pie crust and spread it evenly. Place the pie crust back into the refrigerator while you prepare the haupia layer.
3. **Make the Haupia Layer:**
    - In a medium saucepan, whisk together coconut milk, whole milk, granulated sugar, cornstarch, and salt until smooth.

- Place the saucepan over medium heat and cook, stirring constantly, until the mixture thickens and comes to a gentle boil.
- Continue cooking and stirring for another 1-2 minutes until the haupia is thickened to a pudding-like consistency.
- Remove the saucepan from the heat and stir in vanilla extract.
- Let the haupia mixture cool slightly for about 5-10 minutes.

4. **Assemble the Pie:**
    - Pour the haupia mixture over the chocolate layer in the pie crust, spreading it evenly.
    - Smooth the top with a spatula or back of a spoon.
5. **Chill and Serve:**
    - Refrigerate the Chocolate Haupia Pie for at least 4 hours, or until completely set and chilled.
    - Before serving, you can optionally garnish with whipped cream, chocolate shavings, or toasted coconut flakes.
6. **Slice and Enjoy:**
    - Slice the Chocolate Haupia Pie into wedges and serve chilled.

This Chocolate Haupia Pie is a luscious and creamy dessert that combines the richness of chocolate with the tropical flavor of coconut. It's perfect for special occasions or whenever you want to indulge in a taste of Hawaii's culinary delights! Adjust the sweetness or chocolate intensity according to your preference for a personalized treat.

Lilikoi (Passion Fruit) Cheesecake

Ingredients:

For the Crust:

- 1 1/2 cups graham cracker crumbs
- 1/4 cup granulated sugar
- 1/2 cup unsalted butter, melted

For the Cheesecake Filling:

- 24 oz (three 8 oz packages) cream cheese, softened
- 1 cup granulated sugar
- 3 large eggs
- 1 cup sour cream
- 1/2 cup lilikoi (passion fruit) puree or pulp (strained to remove seeds)
- 1 teaspoon vanilla extract

For the Topping:

- 1/2 cup lilikoi (passion fruit) puree or pulp (strained)
- 1/4 cup granulated sugar
- 1 tablespoon cornstarch
- Fresh fruit or whipped cream for garnish (optional)

Instructions:

1. **Preheat and Prepare:**
   - Preheat your oven to 325°F (160°C). Grease a 9-inch springform pan with butter or cooking spray.
2. **Make the Crust:**
   - In a mixing bowl, combine graham cracker crumbs, sugar, and melted butter until evenly moistened.
   - Press the mixture firmly into the bottom of the prepared springform pan to form the crust. Use the back of a spoon or a measuring cup to compact the crust.
   - Bake the crust in the preheated oven for 10 minutes. Remove from oven and let it cool while you prepare the filling.
3. **Make the Cheesecake Filling:**
   - In a large mixing bowl, beat the softened cream cheese and sugar together until smooth and creamy.
   - Add the eggs one at a time, beating well after each addition.
   - Mix in the sour cream, lilikoi puree, and vanilla extract until smooth and well combined.
4. **Pour and Bake:**

- Pour the cheesecake filling over the cooled crust in the springform pan. Smooth the top with a spatula.

5. **Bake the Cheesecake:**
   - Place the springform pan on a baking sheet (to catch any drips) and bake in the preheated oven for 50-60 minutes, or until the edges are set and the center is slightly jiggly.

6. **Cool and Chill:**
   - Turn off the oven and crack the oven door open. Let the cheesecake cool in the oven for 1 hour.
   - Remove the cheesecake from the oven and let it cool completely at room temperature.
   - Refrigerate the cheesecake for at least 4 hours, or preferably overnight, to chill and set.

7. **Make the Lilikoi Topping:**
   - In a small saucepan, combine lilikoi puree, sugar, and cornstarch. Cook over medium heat, stirring constantly, until the mixture thickens and comes to a boil.
   - Remove from heat and let it cool slightly. Spread the lilikoi topping over the chilled cheesecake.

8. **Serve:**
   - Carefully remove the sides of the springform pan.
   - Slice the Lilikoi Cheesecake into wedges and serve chilled.
   - Garnish with fresh fruit or whipped cream if desired.

This Lilikoi Cheesecake is a tropical delight with its tangy passion fruit flavor complementing the creamy cheesecake. It's a perfect dessert for special occasions or any time you want to indulge in a taste of Hawaii's exotic fruits. Adjust the sweetness or tartness of the lilikoi topping according to your preference for a personalized treat.

Coconut ShrimpHawaiian Sweet Rolls

Ingredients:

- 1 lb large shrimp, peeled and deveined (tails left on or removed, as preferred)
- 1 cup all-purpose flour
- 1/2 teaspoon salt
- 1/4 teaspoon black pepper
- 2 large eggs
- 1 cup shredded coconut (sweetened or unsweetened)
- 1 cup panko breadcrumbs
- Oil for frying (such as vegetable oil or coconut oil)

Instructions:

1. **Prepare the Shrimp:**
   - Pat the shrimp dry with paper towels to remove excess moisture.
2. **Set Up Breading Station:**
   - In one shallow bowl, whisk together the flour, salt, and black pepper.
   - In another shallow bowl, beat the eggs.
3. **Coat the Shrimp:**
   - Dip each shrimp into the flour mixture, shaking off any excess.
   - Next, dip the shrimp into the beaten eggs, allowing any excess to drip off.
   - Finally, coat the shrimp thoroughly in a mixture of shredded coconut and panko breadcrumbs, pressing gently to adhere the coating. Ensure each shrimp is evenly coated.
4. **Fry the Coconut Shrimp:**
   - Heat oil in a large skillet or deep fryer to 350°F (175°C).
   - Carefully place the coated shrimp into the hot oil in batches, making sure not to overcrowd the pan.
   - Fry the shrimp for about 2-3 minutes per side, or until the coating is golden brown and the shrimp is cooked through. The shrimp should be pink and opaque.
   - Remove the cooked shrimp from the oil with a slotted spoon and transfer them to a plate lined with paper towels to drain excess oil.
5. **Serve:**
   - Arrange the Coconut Shrimp on a serving platter.
   - Serve hot with your favorite dipping sauce, such as sweet chili sauce, mango salsa, or a tangy dipping sauce made with lime juice and soy sauce.
6. **Garnish (optional):**
   - Garnish with chopped fresh cilantro or parsley and serve immediately.

Coconut Shrimp is crispy on the outside, tender on the inside, and bursting with tropical flavor from the shredded coconut. It makes for a delightful appetizer or main dish that's sure to impress your family and guests. Adjust the seasoning and frying time based on the size of your shrimp and personal preference for crispiness. Enjoy this delicious taste of the tropics!

Hawaiian Sweet Rolls

Ingredients:

- 1/2 cup pineapple juice
- 1/2 cup whole milk, warmed to about 110°F (45°C)
- 1/4 cup granulated sugar
- 1/4 cup unsalted butter, melted and cooled slightly
- 1 large egg, room temperature
- 4 cups all-purpose flour
- 1 packet (2 1/4 teaspoons) active dry yeast
- 1 teaspoon salt
- 1/4 teaspoon ground nutmeg (optional, for flavor)
- Additional melted butter for brushing

Instructions:

1. **Activate the Yeast:**
    - In a small bowl, combine warm milk, sugar, and yeast. Let it sit for about 5-10 minutes until the yeast becomes foamy.
2. **Mix the Dough:**
    - In a large mixing bowl or the bowl of a stand mixer fitted with a dough hook, combine the activated yeast mixture, pineapple juice, melted butter, and egg.
    - Add 3 cups of flour, salt, and nutmeg (if using). Mix until well combined.
3. **Knead the Dough:**
    - Gradually add the remaining 1 cup of flour, 1/4 cup at a time, until the dough comes together and pulls away from the sides of the bowl.
    - Knead the dough by hand on a lightly floured surface or continue kneading with the dough hook for about 5-7 minutes, until the dough is smooth and elastic.
4. **First Rise:**
    - Place the dough in a greased bowl and cover it with a clean kitchen towel or plastic wrap.
    - Let it rise in a warm, draft-free place for about 1-1.5 hours, or until doubled in size.
5. **Shape the Rolls:**
    - Punch down the risen dough and divide it into 12 equal pieces.
    - Shape each piece into a smooth ball and place them in a greased 9x13-inch baking dish or on a parchment-lined baking sheet, spacing them evenly apart.
6. **Second Rise:**
    - Cover the shaped rolls loosely with a clean kitchen towel or plastic wrap.
    - Let them rise again in a warm place for another 45 minutes to 1 hour, until they have doubled in size and are touching each other.
7. **Bake:**

- Preheat your oven to 350°F (175°C) during the last 15 minutes of the second rise.
- Bake the rolls in the preheated oven for 20-25 minutes, or until they are golden brown on top and sound hollow when tapped.

8. **Finish:**
    - Remove the rolls from the oven and immediately brush the tops with melted butter for a glossy finish.
    - Allow the rolls to cool slightly before serving.

These homemade Hawaiian Sweet Rolls are perfect for sandwiches, sliders, or simply enjoyed warm with butter. Their subtly sweet flavor and soft texture make them a favorite for any occasion. Store any leftovers in an airtight container at room temperature for up to 3 days, or freeze for longer storage. Enjoy the taste of Hawaii right in your own kitchen!

Macadamia Nut Crusted Mahi Mahi

Ingredients:

- 4 mahi mahi fillets (about 6 oz each), skinless
- Salt and pepper, to taste
- 1 cup macadamia nuts, finely chopped or ground
- 1/2 cup panko breadcrumbs
- 1/4 cup all-purpose flour
- 2 large eggs, beaten
- 2 tablespoons Dijon mustard
- 1 tablespoon honey
- 1 tablespoon soy sauce
- 1 tablespoon fresh lime juice
- 2 tablespoons vegetable oil or coconut oil, for cooking

Instructions:

1. **Prepare the Mahi Mahi:**
    - Pat dry the mahi mahi fillets with paper towels. Season both sides with salt and pepper.
2. **Prepare the Coating:**
    - In a shallow bowl or plate, combine the finely chopped macadamia nuts and panko breadcrumbs.
3. **Dredge the Mahi Mahi:**
    - Place the flour on a separate plate.
    - In another shallow bowl, whisk together the beaten eggs.
4. **Coat the Mahi Mahi:**
    - Dredge each mahi mahi fillet in the flour, shaking off any excess.
    - Dip the fillets into the beaten eggs, coating both sides.
5. **Apply the Nut Coating:**
    - Press each side of the mahi mahi fillets into the macadamia nut and breadcrumb mixture, ensuring an even coating.
6. **Make the Glaze:**
    - In a small bowl, whisk together Dijon mustard, honey, soy sauce, and fresh lime juice until well combined.
7. **Cook the Mahi Mahi:**
    - Heat vegetable oil or coconut oil in a large skillet over medium-high heat.
    - Carefully place the coated mahi mahi fillets into the hot skillet. Cook for about 3-4 minutes on each side, or until the nuts are golden brown and the fish flakes easily with a fork.
8. **Serve:**
    - Remove the cooked Mahi Mahi from the skillet and transfer to serving plates.
    - Drizzle the prepared glaze over the fillets before serving.

9. **Garnish (optional):**
    - Garnish with fresh chopped parsley or cilantro, and serve with steamed rice, quinoa, or a fresh salad.

Enjoy this Macadamia Nut Crusted Mahi Mahi as a delicious and satisfying seafood dish that combines the tropical flavors of Hawaii with crunchy macadamia nuts. It's perfect for a special dinner or anytime you want to enjoy a taste of the islands at home!

Huli Huli Ribs

Ingredients:

For the Ribs:

- 2 racks of baby back ribs (about 4-5 lbs total)
- Salt and pepper, to taste
- 2 cloves garlic, minced
- 1 tablespoon grated ginger
- 1/4 cup soy sauce
- 1/4 cup brown sugar
- 1/4 cup pineapple juice
- 1/4 cup ketchup
- 1/4 cup hoisin sauce
- 2 tablespoons rice vinegar
- 2 tablespoons sesame oil
- 1 tablespoon Worcestershire sauce
- 1 tablespoon Sriracha sauce (optional, for heat)
- Sliced green onions and sesame seeds for garnish

Instructions:

1. **Prepare the Ribs:**
   - Preheat your oven to 300°F (150°C).
   - Season the ribs generously with salt and pepper on both sides.
2. **Make the Huli Huli Sauce:**
   - In a bowl, whisk together minced garlic, grated ginger, soy sauce, brown sugar, pineapple juice, ketchup, hoisin sauce, rice vinegar, sesame oil, Worcestershire sauce, and Sriracha sauce (if using). Adjust seasoning to taste.
3. **Marinate the Ribs:**
   - Place the ribs in a large baking dish or a resealable plastic bag.
   - Pour half of the huli huli sauce over the ribs, making sure they are evenly coated. Reserve the remaining sauce for basting later.
   - Cover the dish or seal the bag and marinate the ribs in the refrigerator for at least 4 hours, preferably overnight.
4. **Cook the Ribs:**
   - Remove the ribs from the refrigerator and let them come to room temperature while you preheat the grill.
   - Preheat your grill to medium-high heat (about 375-400°F or 190-200°C).
   - Remove the ribs from the marinade and discard the marinade.
   - Place the ribs on the grill and cook for about 20-25 minutes per side, or until the ribs are cooked through and nicely charred, basting with the reserved huli huli sauce during the last 10 minutes of grilling.

5. **Serve:**
    - Remove the ribs from the grill and let them rest for a few minutes before slicing.
    - Garnish with sliced green onions and sesame seeds.
    - Serve the Huli Huli Ribs hot, accompanied by rice, coleslaw, or your favorite side dishes.

Huli Huli Ribs are a fantastic dish for a barbecue or any gathering, featuring the perfect blend of sweet, tangy, and savory flavors that are synonymous with Hawaiian cuisine. Adjust the level of spiciness with the Sriracha sauce to suit your taste preferences. Enjoy these delicious ribs with friends and family!

Coconut Poke Cake

Ingredients:

For the Cake:

- 1 box (15.25 oz) white cake mix (plus ingredients needed to prepare the cake, such as eggs, oil, and water)
- 1 cup canned coconut milk (full-fat)
- 1/2 cup sweetened condensed milk

For the Topping:

- 1 can (13.5 oz) coconut milk (full-fat)
- 1 can (14 oz) sweetened condensed milk
- 1 cup shredded coconut (sweetened or unsweetened), toasted (optional, for garnish)
- Whipped cream or whipped topping, for serving

Instructions:

1. **Prepare the Cake:**
   - Preheat your oven according to the cake mix package instructions.
   - Grease and flour a 9x13-inch baking dish.
2. **Bake the Cake:**
   - Prepare the white cake mix according to the package instructions, substituting 1 cup of canned coconut milk for the water called for in the instructions.
   - Bake the cake according to the package instructions. Remove from the oven when a toothpick inserted into the center comes out clean.
3. **Poke Holes in the Cake:**
   - While the cake is still warm, use the handle of a wooden spoon or a skewer to poke holes all over the top of the cake. Space the holes evenly.
4. **Make the Coconut Milk Mixture:**
   - In a bowl, mix together the remaining can of coconut milk and 1/2 cup of sweetened condensed milk until well combined.
5. **Pour over the Cake:**
   - Pour the coconut milk mixture evenly over the warm cake, making sure to fill the holes.
   - Allow the cake to cool completely to room temperature. Then, cover and refrigerate for at least 2 hours, or overnight, to allow the flavors to meld and the cake to absorb the coconut milk mixture.
6. **Toast the Coconut (Optional):**
   - If desired, toast the shredded coconut in a dry skillet over medium heat until golden brown and fragrant. Stir frequently to prevent burning.
7. **Serve:**
   - Before serving, spread whipped cream or whipped topping over the chilled cake.

- Sprinkle toasted shredded coconut over the top for garnish, if using.
8. **Slice and Enjoy:**
    - Slice the Coconut Poke Cake into squares and serve chilled. Enjoy the moist and coconut-flavored goodness!

This Coconut Poke Cake is perfect for any occasion, especially for coconut lovers. It's refreshing, creamy, and decadent, making it a delightful treat that's sure to impress. Adjust the sweetness by adding more or less sweetened condensed milk according to your preference. Enjoy this tropical dessert with friends and family!

Ono (Wahoo) Fish Tacos

Ingredients:

For the Ono Fish:

- 1 lb Ono (Wahoo) fish fillets, skinless and boneless
- 1/4 cup olive oil
- Juice of 1 lime
- 2 cloves garlic, minced
- 1 teaspoon ground cumin
- 1 teaspoon chili powder
- Salt and pepper, to taste

For the Slaw:

- 2 cups shredded cabbage (green or purple, or a mix)
- 1/2 cup shredded carrots
- 1/4 cup chopped cilantro
- Juice of 1 lime
- 2 tablespoons mayonnaise
- Salt and pepper, to taste

For Serving:

- 8-10 small flour or corn tortillas
- Sliced avocado or guacamole
- Salsa (store-bought or homemade)
- Lime wedges, for garnish
- Optional: Sour cream, chopped jalapeños, hot sauce

Instructions:

1. **Marinate the Ono Fish:**
   - In a shallow dish, whisk together olive oil, lime juice, minced garlic, ground cumin, chili powder, salt, and pepper.
   - Add the Ono fish fillets to the marinade, turning to coat evenly. Cover and refrigerate for at least 30 minutes, or up to 2 hours.
2. **Make the Slaw:**
   - In a mixing bowl, combine shredded cabbage, shredded carrots, chopped cilantro, lime juice, mayonnaise, salt, and pepper. Toss until well combined. Adjust seasoning to taste.
3. **Cook the Ono Fish:**
   - Preheat your grill or grill pan over medium-high heat.
   - Remove the Ono fish from the marinade and discard the marinade.

- Grill the fish fillets for about 3-4 minutes per side, or until cooked through and flaky. Cooking time may vary depending on the thickness of the fillets.
- Remove the fish from the grill and let it rest for a few minutes. Then, flake the fish into large chunks with a fork.

4. **Assemble the Tacos:**
    - Warm the tortillas in a dry skillet or directly over the flame of a gas burner until lightly charred and pliable.
    - Place a spoonful of the slaw on each tortilla.
    - Top with flaked Ono fish.
    - Add sliced avocado or guacamole, salsa, and any additional toppings you desire (sour cream, jalapeños, hot sauce).
    - Garnish with lime wedges.

5. **Serve:**
    - Serve the Ono Fish Tacos immediately, with extra lime wedges on the side for squeezing over the tacos.
    - Enjoy the fresh flavors and textures of these delicious Ono Fish Tacos!

These Ono Fish Tacos are perfect for a light and flavorful meal, combining the delicate flavor of Ono fish with the crunch of slaw and the creaminess of avocado. Customize the toppings and seasonings according to your taste preferences for a truly enjoyable dining experience!

Punalu'u Sweet Bread

Ingredients:

- 3 ripe bananas (or substitute with 1 cup mashed taro or sweet potato)
- 1/2 cup unsalted butter, melted and cooled slightly
- 1/2 cup granulated sugar
- 1/2 cup brown sugar
- 2 large eggs
- 1 teaspoon vanilla extract
- 1/2 cup buttermilk (or substitute with regular milk mixed with 1/2 tablespoon vinegar)
- 2 cups all-purpose flour
- 1 teaspoon baking powder
- 1/2 teaspoon baking soda
- 1/2 teaspoon salt
- Optional: 1/2 cup chopped macadamia nuts or shredded coconut for added texture and flavor

Instructions:

1. **Preheat and Prepare:**
   - Preheat your oven to 350°F (175°C). Grease and flour a 9x5-inch loaf pan.
2. **Prepare the Banana (or Taro) Mixture:**
   - If using bananas, mash them in a bowl until smooth. If using taro or sweet potato, cook and mash them until smooth.
   - Mix in the melted butter, granulated sugar, and brown sugar until well combined.
3. **Add Wet Ingredients:**
   - Beat in the eggs one at a time, followed by the vanilla extract and buttermilk. Mix until smooth.
4. **Combine Dry Ingredients:**
   - In a separate bowl, whisk together the flour, baking powder, baking soda, and salt.
5. **Combine Wet and Dry Ingredients:**
   - Gradually add the dry ingredients to the wet ingredients, mixing until just combined. Be careful not to overmix.
   - If using, fold in the chopped macadamia nuts or shredded coconut.
6. **Bake the Bread:**
   - Pour the batter into the prepared loaf pan, spreading it evenly.
   - Bake in the preheated oven for 50-60 minutes, or until a toothpick inserted into the center comes out clean.
7. **Cool and Serve:**
   - Allow the bread to cool in the pan for 10-15 minutes before transferring it to a wire rack to cool completely.

- Once cooled, slice and serve the Punalu'u Sweet Bread. Enjoy it warm or at room temperature.

This Punalu'u Sweet Bread is perfect for breakfast, brunch, or as a snack any time of day. The addition of bananas, taro, or sweet potato gives it a unique Hawaiian twist, while the texture is moist and tender. Serve it plain or with a smear of butter for a delightful treat that captures the flavors of Hawaii.

Chicken Katsu

Ingredients:

For the Chicken:

- 4 boneless, skinless chicken breasts (about 1.5 lbs)
- Salt and pepper, to taste
- 1/2 cup all-purpose flour
- 2 large eggs, beaten
- 1 cup panko breadcrumbs (Japanese breadcrumbs)
- Vegetable oil, for frying

For the Tonkatsu Sauce:

- 1/2 cup ketchup
- 2 tablespoons Worcestershire sauce
- 1 tablespoon soy sauce
- 1 tablespoon sugar
- 1 teaspoon Dijon mustard
- 1 clove garlic, minced (optional)

For Serving:

- Cooked rice
- Shredded cabbage (optional)
- Lemon wedges

Instructions:

1. **Prepare the Chicken:**
   - Place each chicken breast between sheets of plastic wrap and pound to an even thickness (about 1/2 inch thick). This helps the chicken cook evenly and tenderizes it.
   - Season both sides of the chicken breasts with salt and pepper.
2. **Set Up Breading Station:**
   - Prepare three shallow dishes: one with flour, one with beaten eggs, and one with panko breadcrumbs.
3. **Bread the Chicken:**
   - Dredge each chicken breast in flour, shaking off any excess.
   - Dip the chicken into the beaten eggs, coating both sides.
   - Press the chicken into the panko breadcrumbs, ensuring an even coating. Press gently to adhere the breadcrumbs.
4. **Fry the Chicken:**

- Heat vegetable oil in a large skillet over medium heat, or use a deep fryer if preferred.
- Carefully place the breaded chicken breasts into the hot oil, cooking 3-4 minutes per side, or until golden brown and cooked through (internal temperature should reach 165°F or 75°C).
- Remove the chicken from the oil and transfer to a wire rack or paper towels to drain excess oil.

5. **Make the Tonkatsu Sauce:**
    - In a small saucepan, combine ketchup, Worcestershire sauce, soy sauce, sugar, Dijon mustard, and minced garlic (if using). Bring to a simmer over medium heat, stirring occasionally, for about 3-5 minutes until slightly thickened. Remove from heat.
6. **Serve:**
    - Slice the Chicken Katsu into strips or leave whole.
    - Serve with steamed rice, shredded cabbage (if using), and tonkatsu sauce on the side.
    - Garnish with lemon wedges for squeezing over the chicken.
7. **Enjoy:**
    - Enjoy the Chicken Katsu while hot and crispy, dipping each bite into the tangy tonkatsu sauce for extra flavor.

Chicken Katsu is a delicious and comforting dish that is sure to be a hit at the dinner table. It's crispy on the outside, tender and juicy on the inside, and pairs perfectly with the savory tonkatsu sauce. Serve it with a side of rice and shredded cabbage for a complete meal that will satisfy everyone's taste buds.

Hawaiian Style Chili

Ingredients:

- 1 lb ground beef (or ground turkey)
- 1 onion, chopped
- 3 cloves garlic, minced
- 1 bell pepper, chopped (any color)
- 1 can (15 oz) kidney beans, drained and rinsed
- 1 can (15 oz) black beans, drained and rinsed
- 1 can (15 oz) diced tomatoes
- 1 can (6 oz) tomato paste
- 2 cups beef broth or chicken broth
- 1 tablespoon chili powder
- 1 teaspoon ground cumin
- 1 teaspoon paprika
- 1/2 teaspoon dried oregano
- 1/2 teaspoon garlic powder
- Salt and pepper, to taste
- 1 tablespoon vegetable oil
- Optional toppings: shredded cheese, sour cream, sliced jalapeños, chopped cilantro

Instructions:

1. **Brown the Ground Beef:**
   - Heat vegetable oil in a large pot or Dutch oven over medium-high heat.
   - Add ground beef (or turkey) and cook until browned, breaking it up with a spoon as it cooks. Drain any excess fat.
2. **Cook the Aromatics:**
   - Add chopped onion, minced garlic, and chopped bell pepper to the pot with the browned meat. Cook for 5-7 minutes, or until the vegetables are softened.
3. **Add Beans and Tomatoes:**
   - Stir in drained and rinsed kidney beans, black beans, diced tomatoes, and tomato paste.
4. **Season the Chili:**
   - Add chili powder, ground cumin, paprika, dried oregano, garlic powder, salt, and pepper to the pot. Stir well to combine all ingredients.
5. **Simmer:**
   - Pour in beef broth or chicken broth, stirring to combine.
   - Bring the chili to a boil, then reduce heat to low. Cover and simmer for 30-40 minutes, stirring occasionally, to allow the flavors to meld and the chili to thicken.
6. **Adjust Seasoning:**
   - Taste and adjust seasoning with more salt and pepper if needed.
7. **Serve:**

        - Ladle the Hawaiian Style Chili into bowls.
        - Garnish with shredded cheese, sour cream, sliced jalapeños, and chopped cilantro as desired.
8. **Enjoy:**
        - Serve the Hawaiian Style Chili hot, accompanied by rice, cornbread, or tortilla chips for a delicious and comforting meal.

This Hawaiian Style Chili is rich, hearty, and packed with flavor, making it a perfect dish for cooler evenings or gatherings with friends and family. Adjust the spice level by adding more or less chili powder and jalapeños according to your preference. It's a versatile dish that can be customized to suit your taste while offering a taste of the islands with every bite.

Mango Bread

Ingredients:

- 2 cups all-purpose flour
- 1 teaspoon baking powder
- 1/2 teaspoon baking soda
- 1/2 teaspoon salt
- 1 teaspoon ground cinnamon
- 1/2 cup unsalted butter, melted and cooled slightly
- 3/4 cup granulated sugar
- 2 large eggs
- 1 teaspoon vanilla extract
- 1 1/2 cups ripe mango, diced (about 2 medium-sized mangoes)
- 1/2 cup chopped walnuts or pecans (optional)
- 1/4 cup shredded coconut (optional)

Instructions:

1. **Preheat and Prepare:**
   - Preheat your oven to 350°F (175°C). Grease and flour a 9x5-inch loaf pan or line it with parchment paper for easy removal.
2. **Dry Ingredients:**
   - In a medium bowl, whisk together the flour, baking powder, baking soda, salt, and ground cinnamon. Set aside.
3. **Wet Ingredients:**
   - In a large mixing bowl, whisk together the melted butter and granulated sugar until well combined.
   - Add the eggs one at a time, whisking well after each addition.
   - Stir in the vanilla extract.
4. **Combine and Mix:**
   - Gradually add the dry ingredients to the wet ingredients, mixing until just combined. Be careful not to overmix.
   - Gently fold in the diced mango and chopped nuts (if using) until evenly distributed in the batter.
5. **Bake the Bread:**
   - Pour the batter into the prepared loaf pan, spreading it evenly.
   - If using shredded coconut, sprinkle it evenly over the top of the batter.
6. **Bake:**
   - Bake in the preheated oven for 55-65 minutes, or until a toothpick inserted into the center comes out clean or with a few moist crumbs attached.
7. **Cool:**
   - Allow the Mango Bread to cool in the pan for 10-15 minutes.
   - Remove from the pan and transfer to a wire rack to cool completely.

8. **Serve:**
    - Slice the Mango Bread and serve it plain or with a spread of butter.
    - Enjoy the tropical flavors of mango in this moist and delicious quick bread!

This Mango Bread is perfect for breakfast, brunch, or as a sweet snack. It captures the essence of fresh mangoes with a hint of cinnamon and nuts, making it a delightful treat any time of year. Store any leftovers in an airtight container at room temperature for up to 3 days, or freeze for longer storage.

Kalbi Ribs

Ingredients:

- 3 lbs beef short ribs, cut crosswise into thin strips (about 1/4 to 1/2 inch thick)
- 1/2 cup soy sauce
- 1/4 cup brown sugar
- 1/4 cup mirin (Japanese sweet rice wine) or dry white wine
- 3 tablespoons sesame oil
- 3 tablespoons rice vinegar
- 4 cloves garlic, minced
- 1 small onion, grated
- 1 tablespoon grated fresh ginger
- 2 green onions, chopped (green and white parts)
- 1 tablespoon toasted sesame seeds
- Freshly ground black pepper, to taste

Instructions:

1. **Prepare the Marinade:**
    - In a bowl, whisk together soy sauce, brown sugar, mirin (or white wine), sesame oil, rice vinegar, minced garlic, grated onion, grated ginger, chopped green onions, sesame seeds, and black pepper.
2. **Marinate the Ribs:**
    - Place the beef short ribs in a large resealable plastic bag or a shallow dish.
    - Pour the marinade over the ribs, making sure they are well coated.
    - Seal the bag or cover the dish with plastic wrap and marinate in the refrigerator for at least 4 hours, or overnight for best results. Turn the ribs occasionally to ensure even marination.
3. **Grill the Ribs:**
    - Preheat your grill to medium-high heat.
    - Remove the ribs from the marinade, shaking off any excess marinade.
    - Grill the ribs for about 3-4 minutes per side, or until they are nicely charred and cooked to your desired doneness. Cooking time may vary depending on the thickness of the ribs.
4. **Serve:**
    - Transfer the grilled Kalbi Ribs to a serving platter.
    - Garnish with additional chopped green onions and sesame seeds, if desired.
    - Serve hot with steamed rice and your favorite Korean side dishes like kimchi or pickled vegetables.
5. **Enjoy:**
    - Enjoy the tender and flavorful Kalbi Ribs straight from the grill, savoring the delicious blend of savory, sweet, and tangy flavors from the marinade.

Kalbi Ribs are a fantastic dish for a barbecue or any gathering, offering a taste of Korean cuisine with its distinctive marinade and grilled goodness. Adjust the sweetness or saltiness of the marinade to suit your taste preferences. This dish is sure to be a hit with family and friends!

Coconut Butter Mochi

Ingredients:

- 1/2 cup unsalted butter, melted and cooled
- 1 can (14 oz) coconut milk (full-fat)
- 4 large eggs
- 2 cups granulated sugar
- 1 teaspoon vanilla extract
- 2 cups mochiko (sweet rice flour)
- 1 teaspoon baking powder
- 1 cup shredded coconut (sweetened or unsweetened)

Instructions:

1. **Preheat and Prepare:**
   - Preheat your oven to 350°F (175°C). Grease a 9x13-inch baking dish or line it with parchment paper for easier removal.
2. **Mix Wet Ingredients:**
   - In a large bowl, whisk together melted butter, coconut milk, eggs, sugar, and vanilla extract until well combined.
3. **Add Dry Ingredients:**
   - Gradually add mochiko and baking powder to the wet ingredients, stirring until smooth and no lumps remain.
4. **Incorporate Coconut:**
   - Fold in shredded coconut until evenly distributed throughout the batter.
5. **Bake:**
   - Pour the batter into the prepared baking dish, spreading it evenly with a spatula.
6. **Bake the Mochi:**
   - Bake in the preheated oven for 50-60 minutes, or until the top is golden brown and the edges are slightly crispy. The center should be set but still slightly soft.
7. **Cool and Serve:**
   - Allow the Coconut Butter Mochi to cool completely in the baking dish.
   - Once cooled, slice into squares or rectangles and serve.
8. **Enjoy:**
   - Serve Coconut Butter Mochi at room temperature as a delicious dessert or snack. It can be enjoyed on its own or with a dusting of powdered sugar on top.

This Coconut Butter Mochi recipe yields a chewy and flavorful treat that captures the essence of coconut in every bite. It's a favorite dessert in Hawaii and perfect for sharing with friends and family. Store any leftovers in an airtight container at room temperature for up to a few days, though it's best enjoyed fresh.

Garlic Shrimp

Ingredients:

- 1 lb large shrimp, peeled and deveined
- 4 tablespoons unsalted butter
- 4 cloves garlic, minced
- 1/4 teaspoon red pepper flakes (optional, for heat)
- Salt and pepper, to taste
- 2 tablespoons fresh parsley, chopped
- 1 tablespoon lemon juice
- Lemon wedges, for serving
- Cooked rice or crusty bread, for serving

Instructions:

1. **Prepare the Shrimp:**
    - Pat the shrimp dry with paper towels and season with salt and pepper.
2. **Cook the Garlic Shrimp:**
    - In a large skillet or frying pan, melt the butter over medium-high heat.
    - Add minced garlic and red pepper flakes (if using) to the skillet. Cook for about 1 minute, stirring constantly, until the garlic is fragrant and just starting to brown.
3. **Add the Shrimp:**
    - Add the seasoned shrimp to the skillet in a single layer. Cook for 2-3 minutes per side, or until the shrimp turn pink and opaque. Be careful not to overcook the shrimp as they can become tough.
4. **Finish the Dish:**
    - Remove the skillet from heat. Stir in chopped parsley and lemon juice, tossing to coat the shrimp evenly with the garlic butter sauce.
5. **Serve:**
    - Serve the Garlic Shrimp hot, garnished with additional parsley and lemon wedges.
    - Serve over cooked rice or with crusty bread to soak up the delicious garlic butter sauce.
6. **Enjoy:**
    - Enjoy the Garlic Shrimp immediately while hot and flavorful. It's perfect for a quick and satisfying meal with a touch of Hawaiian flair.

This Garlic Shrimp recipe is quick and easy to prepare, making it ideal for weeknight dinners or when you want to enjoy a taste of Hawaii at home. Adjust the amount of garlic and red pepper flakes to suit your taste preferences for a dish that's just right for you.

Pineapple Upside-Down Cake

Ingredients:

For the topping:

- 1/4 cup unsalted butter
- 3/4 cup packed light brown sugar
- 1 can (20 oz) pineapple slices in juice, drained (reserve juice)
- Maraschino cherries, drained (optional)

For the cake:

- 1 1/2 cups all-purpose flour
- 2 teaspoons baking powder
- 1/4 teaspoon salt
- 1/2 cup unsalted butter, softened
- 1 cup granulated sugar
- 2 large eggs
- 1 teaspoon vanilla extract
- 1/2 cup pineapple juice (reserved from canned pineapple)
- 1/4 cup buttermilk (or substitute with regular milk mixed with 1/2 tablespoon vinegar)

Instructions:

1. **Preheat and Prepare:**
   - Preheat your oven to 350°F (175°C). Grease a 9-inch round cake pan.
2. **Make the topping:**
   - Melt the 1/4 cup of butter in a small saucepan over medium heat.
   - Stir in the brown sugar until dissolved and bubbling, about 2-3 minutes.
   - Pour the mixture into the greased cake pan, spreading it evenly.
   - Arrange pineapple slices on top of the brown sugar mixture. Place a cherry in the center of each pineapple slice, if using.
3. **Prepare the cake batter:**
   - In a medium bowl, whisk together flour, baking powder, and salt. Set aside.
   - In a large bowl, beat the softened butter and granulated sugar until light and fluffy.
   - Add eggs one at a time, beating well after each addition.
   - Stir in vanilla extract.
   - Gradually add the flour mixture to the butter mixture, alternating with pineapple juice and buttermilk, beginning and ending with the flour mixture. Mix until just combined.
4. **Assemble and bake:**
   - Carefully spread the cake batter over the pineapple slices in the cake pan, smoothing the top with a spatula.

- Bake in the preheated oven for 45-50 minutes, or until a toothpick inserted into the center comes out clean.

5. **Cool and invert:**
    - Remove the cake from the oven and let it cool in the pan for 10 minutes.
    - Place a serving plate upside down over the cake pan, then carefully invert the cake onto the plate. Allow the pan to sit on the inverted cake for a few minutes to let the caramel topping drizzle down.
6. **Serve:**
    - Serve the Pineapple Upside-Down Cake warm or at room temperature.
    - Optionally, garnish with whipped cream or vanilla ice cream.
7. **Enjoy:**
    - Enjoy the delicious combination of caramelized pineapple, sweet cherries, and moist cake in this classic dessert!

This Pineapple Upside-Down Cake is perfect for any occasion, bringing a taste of tropical sweetness to your table. It's a timeless dessert that's sure to please everyone's taste buds.

Teriyaki Beef Skewers

Ingredients:

- 1 lb beef sirloin or flank steak, cut into 1-inch cubes
- Bamboo skewers, soaked in water for 30 minutes (to prevent burning)
- 1/2 cup soy sauce
- 1/4 cup mirin (Japanese sweet rice wine)
- 2 tablespoons brown sugar
- 2 cloves garlic, minced
- 1 tablespoon grated fresh ginger
- 2 tablespoons sesame oil
- 1 tablespoon cornstarch (optional, for thickening)
- Sesame seeds and chopped green onions, for garnish

Instructions:

1. **Prepare the Marinade:**
   - In a bowl, whisk together soy sauce, mirin, brown sugar, minced garlic, grated ginger, and sesame oil until well combined.
2. **Marinate the Beef:**
   - Place the cubed beef in a shallow dish or resealable plastic bag.
   - Pour the marinade over the beef, making sure it is evenly coated. Marinate in the refrigerator for at least 30 minutes, or up to 2 hours for more flavor.
3. **Prepare the Skewers:**
   - Preheat your grill to medium-high heat, or preheat your broiler.
4. **Skewer the Beef:**
   - Thread the marinated beef cubes onto the soaked bamboo skewers, leaving a little space between each piece.
5. **Grill or Broil:**
   - Grill the skewers for about 3-4 minutes per side, or until the beef is cooked to your desired doneness and has nice grill marks.
   - Alternatively, broil the skewers in the oven for about 4-5 minutes per side, until the beef is cooked through and caramelized.
6. **Optional: Make a Glaze (Cornstarch Slurry):**
   - If desired, you can thicken the remaining marinade to make a glaze. In a small saucepan, combine the leftover marinade with 1 tablespoon of cornstarch dissolved in 2 tablespoons of water. Bring to a boil, stirring constantly, until the sauce thickens.
7. **Serve:**
   - Remove the Teriyaki Beef Skewers from the grill or broiler.
   - Brush the skewers with the optional glaze (if using) or drizzle any remaining marinade over them.
   - Sprinkle with sesame seeds and chopped green onions for garnish.

8. **Enjoy:**
    - Serve the Teriyaki Beef Skewers hot as a main dish or as part of a meal with rice and steamed vegetables.

These Teriyaki Beef Skewers are tender, juicy, and full of savory-sweet teriyaki flavor. They're perfect for a barbecue or any occasion where you want to enjoy delicious grilled beef with a touch of Asian-inspired marinade. Adjust the sweetness or saltiness of the marinade to suit your taste preferences for a dish that's sure to be a hit!

Banana Lumpia

Ingredients:

- 6 ripe bananas (preferably saba or plantains)
- 12 spring roll wrappers (also known as lumpia wrappers)
- 1 cup brown sugar
- 1/2 cup jackfruit strips (optional, for added flavor)
- Vegetable oil, for frying

Instructions:

1. **Prepare the Bananas:**
   - Peel the bananas and cut each one in half crosswise. You should have 12 pieces in total.
2. **Assemble the Lumpia:**
   - Lay a spring roll wrapper on a clean surface with one corner pointing towards you (diamond shape).
   - Place a banana piece horizontally on the wrapper, slightly above the bottom corner.
   - Optional: Add a few strips of jackfruit alongside the banana for extra flavor.
3. **Roll the Lumpia:**
   - Fold the bottom corner of the wrapper over the banana.
   - Fold in the sides towards the center, then roll up tightly towards the top corner to enclose the banana completely.
   - Moisten the top corner with water to seal the lumpia. Repeat with the remaining bananas and wrappers.
4. **Fry the Lumpia:**
   - Heat vegetable oil in a deep frying pan or pot over medium heat, enough to submerge the lumpia.
   - Carefully place the lumpia in the hot oil, seam side down, a few at a time to avoid overcrowding.
   - Fry for about 3-4 minutes per side, or until the lumpia are golden brown and crispy.
   - Remove with a slotted spoon and drain on paper towels to remove excess oil.
5. **Serve:**
   - Serve the Banana Lumpia warm.
   - Optionally, sprinkle with brown sugar or drizzle with caramel sauce before serving for added sweetness.
6. **Enjoy:**
   - Enjoy the crispy and caramelized Banana Lumpia as a delicious snack or dessert. They are best eaten fresh and warm.

Banana Lumpia (Turon) is a popular Filipino treat enjoyed for its crunchy exterior and sweet, soft banana filling. It's perfect for parties or gatherings and can be served with ice cream or enjoyed on its own. Adjust the sweetness by adding more or less sugar according to your preference.

Taro Smoothie

Ingredients:

- 1 cup cooked and mashed taro root (cooled)
- 1 cup milk (dairy or non-dairy such as almond milk or coconut milk)
- 1 tablespoon honey or sweetener of choice (adjust to taste)
- 1/2 cup plain yogurt (optional, for added creaminess)
- 1/2 teaspoon vanilla extract
- Ice cubes (optional, for a colder smoothie)

Instructions:

1. **Prepare the Taro:**
   - Cook taro root until tender. Peel and mash it until smooth. Let it cool completely before using in the smoothie.
2. **Blend the Ingredients:**
   - In a blender, combine the mashed taro root, milk, honey (or sweetener), yogurt (if using), and vanilla extract.
   - Optionally, add a handful of ice cubes for a colder smoothie.
3. **Blend until Smooth:**
   - Blend all ingredients until smooth and creamy. If the smoothie is too thick, add more milk until desired consistency is reached.
4. **Serve:**
   - Pour the Taro Smoothie into glasses.
   - Garnish with a sprinkle of ground cinnamon or a slice of taro root for decoration, if desired.
5. **Enjoy:**
   - Serve the Taro Smoothie immediately and enjoy the creamy, subtly sweet flavor of taro root.

Taro Smoothies are a delightful way to experience the unique flavor and creamy texture of taro root. They are perfect for breakfast, a snack, or a refreshing drink on a warm day. Feel free to adjust the sweetness and consistency of the smoothie to suit your taste preferences.

Hawaiian Plate Lunch

Components of a Hawaiian Plate Lunch:

1. **Protein Options:**
    - **Kalua Pig:** Tender, smoky shredded pork traditionally cooked in an underground oven called an imu.
    - **Laulau:** Steamed bundles of pork or fish wrapped in taro leaves.
    - **Chicken Katsu:** Breaded and fried chicken cutlets served with a tangy sauce.
    - **Teriyaki Beef or Chicken:** Grilled beef or chicken marinated in a sweet teriyaki sauce.
    - **Loco Moco:** A popular dish with a hamburger patty topped with a fried egg and brown gravy.
    - **Garlic Shrimp:** Shrimp cooked in garlic and butter, often served with rice.
2. **Starch Component:**
    - **White Rice:** Typically steamed and served alongside the protein.
    - **Macaroni Salad:** A creamy and tangy pasta salad with mayonnaise, often mixed with vegetables like carrots and celery.
    - **Potato Mac Salad:** A combination of potato salad and macaroni salad.
3. **Side Dishes:**
    - **Lomi Lomi Salmon:** A traditional Hawaiian side dish made with salted salmon, tomatoes, onions, and sometimes chili peppers.
    - **Poi:** A staple Hawaiian starch made from mashed taro root.
    - **Hawaiian Sweet Rolls:** Soft and slightly sweet bread rolls, often served with butter.
4. **Condiments and Sauces:**
    - **Shoyu (Soy Sauce) and Furikake:** Used as seasoning for rice.
    - **Pineapple Slices:** Sometimes served as a refreshing side or garnish.
    - **Soy Sauce or Teriyaki Sauce:** For drizzling over meats or rice.

Serving a Hawaiian Plate Lunch:

- Each component is usually served in generous portions on a single plate, creating a balanced and satisfying meal.
- It's common for plate lunches to be served with additional condiments or sauces on the side for diners to customize their meal to their liking.
- The combination of savory meats, starches, and sides reflects the diverse culinary influences in Hawaii, blending traditional Hawaiian flavors with Asian and American cuisines.

Hawaiian Plate Lunches are not only a delicious meal but also a cultural experience, offering a taste of Hawaii's rich culinary heritage and local flavors.

Coconut Shrimp Curry

Ingredients:

- 1 lb large shrimp, peeled and deveined
- 1 tablespoon vegetable oil
- 1 onion, finely chopped
- 3 cloves garlic, minced
- 1 tablespoon fresh ginger, grated
- 1 red bell pepper, sliced
- 1 tablespoon curry powder
- 1 teaspoon ground turmeric
- 1 can (14 oz) coconut milk
- 1 tablespoon fish sauce (optional, for extra umami)
- 1 tablespoon brown sugar or honey (adjust to taste)
- Salt and pepper, to taste
- Fresh cilantro or parsley, chopped (for garnish)
- Cooked rice, for serving

Instructions:

1. **Prepare the Shrimp:**
   - Pat the shrimp dry with paper towels. Season with salt and pepper.
2. **Sauté the Aromatics:**
   - Heat the vegetable oil in a large skillet or pan over medium heat.
   - Add the chopped onion and cook until softened and translucent, about 3-4 minutes.
   - Stir in the minced garlic and grated ginger, cooking for another 1-2 minutes until fragrant.
3. **Add Spices:**
   - Sprinkle curry powder and ground turmeric over the onion mixture. Stir well to combine and cook for about 1 minute to toast the spices.
4. **Simmer with Coconut Milk:**
   - Pour in the coconut milk, stirring to combine with the onion and spice mixture.
   - Bring the mixture to a simmer and cook for 5 minutes, allowing the flavors to meld together.
5. **Add Shrimp:**
   - Add the seasoned shrimp to the skillet, stirring to coat them in the curry sauce.
   - Cook the shrimp for 5-6 minutes, or until they are pink and opaque, stirring occasionally.
6. **Adjust Seasoning:**
   - Taste the curry and adjust seasoning as needed with fish sauce, brown sugar (or honey), salt, and pepper. The fish sauce adds depth of flavor, but you can omit it if preferred.

7. **Serve:**
    - Serve the Coconut Shrimp Curry hot over cooked rice.
    - Garnish with chopped cilantro or parsley for freshness.
8. **Enjoy:**
    - Enjoy the creamy and aromatic Coconut Shrimp Curry with rice, soaking up the flavorful sauce. It's a comforting and satisfying dish with a tropical twist!

This Coconut Shrimp Curry recipe is versatile and can be adjusted based on your spice preferences. Feel free to add more vegetables like spinach or peas for extra nutrition and color. It's perfect for a weeknight dinner or when you're craving a taste of exotic flavors at home.

Haupia Ice Cream

Ingredients:

- 1 can (14 oz) coconut milk (full-fat)
- 1 cup whole milk (or substitute with coconut milk for a richer flavor)
- 1/2 cup granulated sugar
- 1/4 cup cornstarch
- 1/4 teaspoon salt
- 1 teaspoon vanilla extract
- Optional: shredded coconut for texture

Instructions:

1. **Prepare the Haupia Base:**
   - In a saucepan, whisk together the coconut milk, whole milk (or additional coconut milk), sugar, cornstarch, and salt over medium heat.
2. **Cook the Mixture:**
   - Cook the mixture, stirring constantly, until it thickens and comes to a gentle boil (about 5-7 minutes).
   - Reduce heat and simmer for an additional 2-3 minutes, continuing to stir until the mixture is smooth and thickened.
3. **Add Vanilla and Coconut (optional):**
   - Remove the saucepan from heat and stir in the vanilla extract.
   - If desired, stir in shredded coconut for added texture and flavor.
4. **Cool the Haupia Base:**
   - Transfer the haupia mixture to a bowl and let it cool to room temperature. Then cover and refrigerate until chilled (at least 4 hours or overnight).
5. **Churn the Ice Cream:**
   - Once chilled, pour the haupia mixture into an ice cream maker and churn according to the manufacturer's instructions until it reaches a soft-serve consistency.
6. **Freeze the Ice Cream:**
   - Transfer the churned ice cream to a freezer-safe container.
   - Cover and freeze for at least 4 hours, or until firm.
7. **Serve:**
   - Scoop the Haupia Ice Cream into bowls or cones.
   - Garnish with toasted coconut flakes or fresh fruit, if desired.
8. **Enjoy:**
   - Enjoy the creamy and coconutty flavor of Haupia Ice Cream as a refreshing dessert or treat.

This Haupia Ice Cream recipe captures the essence of traditional Hawaiian haupia in a delightful frozen form. It's perfect for enjoying on its own or as a complement to other tropical desserts. Adjust the sweetness and texture to suit your preferences for a personalized ice cream experience at home.

Hawaiian Style Potato Salad

Ingredients:

- 2 lbs potatoes (Yukon Gold or red potatoes work well), peeled and cut into 1-inch cubes
- 3 hard-boiled eggs, peeled and chopped
- 1 cup mayonnaise
- 1 tablespoon apple cider vinegar (or rice vinegar)
- 1 tablespoon soy sauce
- 1 tablespoon Dijon mustard
- 1/2 cup chopped celery
- 1/2 cup chopped red bell pepper
- 1/4 cup chopped green onions
- Salt and pepper, to taste
- Optional: 1/2 cup chopped pineapple (for a touch of sweetness)

Instructions:

1. **Cook the Potatoes:**
   - Place the cubed potatoes in a large pot and cover with water. Bring to a boil over medium-high heat.
   - Reduce heat to medium-low and simmer for 10-15 minutes, or until the potatoes are fork-tender.
   - Drain the potatoes and let them cool slightly.
2. **Prepare the Dressing:**
   - In a large bowl, whisk together mayonnaise, apple cider vinegar, soy sauce, and Dijon mustard until smooth and well combined.
3. **Assemble the Salad:**
   - Add the cooled potatoes, chopped hard-boiled eggs, chopped celery, chopped red bell pepper, and chopped green onions to the bowl with the dressing.
   - If using, add chopped pineapple for a touch of sweetness.
   - Gently toss everything together until the ingredients are evenly coated with the dressing.
   - Season with salt and pepper to taste.
4. **Chill and Serve:**
   - Cover the Hawaiian Style Potato Salad and refrigerate for at least 1 hour to allow the flavors to meld together.
5. **Enjoy:**
   - Serve chilled as a side dish or as part of a Hawaiian plate lunch.
   - Garnish with additional chopped green onions or a sprinkle of paprika, if desired.

This Hawaiian Style Potato Salad is creamy, slightly sweet, and packed with flavor from the combination of ingredients. It's perfect for picnics, barbecues, or any occasion where you want to bring a taste of Hawaii to the table. Adjust the ingredients and seasonings according to your preferences for a personalized twist on this classic dish.

Lomi Salmon Salad

Ingredients:

- 1 lb salted salmon (or substitute with smoked salmon), skin removed and diced
- 4 ripe tomatoes, seeded and diced
- 1 small sweet onion, finely diced
- 2 green onions, thinly sliced
- 1 teaspoon crushed red pepper flakes (optional, for a spicy kick)
- Juice of 1-2 limes (adjust to taste)
- Freshly ground black pepper, to taste
- Fresh cilantro or parsley, chopped (for garnish)
- Cooked white rice, for serving (optional)

Instructions:

1. **Prepare the Salmon:**
   - If using salted salmon, soak it in cold water for about 1 hour to remove excess salt. Drain well and pat dry with paper towels. Remove the skin and dice the salmon into small pieces.
   - If using smoked salmon, simply dice it into small pieces.
2. **Combine Ingredients:**
   - In a large bowl, combine the diced salmon, diced tomatoes, finely diced sweet onion, sliced green onions, and crushed red pepper flakes (if using).
3. **Season the Salad:**
   - Squeeze lime juice over the salad mixture. Start with juice from 1 lime and adjust to taste.
   - Season with freshly ground black pepper to taste. Avoid adding additional salt if using salted salmon, as it is already salty.
4. **Mix and Chill:**
   - Gently toss all the ingredients together until well combined.
   - Cover the bowl with plastic wrap and refrigerate for at least 30 minutes to allow the flavors to meld together.
5. **Serve:**
   - Serve Lomi Lomi Salmon Salad chilled as a side dish or appetizer.
   - Optionally, garnish with chopped cilantro or parsley for added freshness.
   - Serve with cooked white rice if desired, to enjoy as a main course.
6. **Enjoy:**
   - Enjoy the refreshing and tangy flavors of Lomi Lomi Salmon Salad, which is perfect for a taste of authentic Hawaiian cuisine at home. It's light, flavorful, and ideal for warm weather gatherings or as part of a Hawaiian meal spread. Adjust the ingredients and seasoning according to your taste preferences for a personalized touch.

Poi Pancakes

Ingredients:

- 1 cup all-purpose flour
- 1/2 cup poi (traditional Hawaiian taro root paste)
- 2 tablespoons sugar
- 1 teaspoon baking powder
- 1/2 teaspoon baking soda
- 1/4 teaspoon salt
- 1 cup buttermilk (or 1 cup milk mixed with 1 tablespoon vinegar or lemon juice)
- 1 large egg
- 2 tablespoons unsalted butter, melted
- Cooking spray or additional butter for cooking

Instructions:

1. **Prepare the Dry Ingredients:**
   - In a large bowl, whisk together the flour, sugar, baking powder, baking soda, and salt.
2. **Mix Wet Ingredients:**
   - In another bowl, whisk together the poi, buttermilk, egg, and melted butter until well combined.
3. **Combine Wet and Dry Ingredients:**
   - Pour the wet ingredients into the bowl with the dry ingredients. Stir gently until just combined. The batter may be slightly lumpy, but avoid overmixing.
4. **Preheat the Griddle or Pan:**
   - Preheat a griddle or non-stick frying pan over medium heat. Lightly grease the surface with cooking spray or butter.
5. **Cook the Pancakes:**
   - Pour about 1/4 cup of batter onto the preheated griddle for each pancake. Use the back of a spoon or measuring cup to spread the batter into a round shape, if needed.
6. **Cook Until Golden Brown:**
   - Cook the pancakes for 2-3 minutes, or until bubbles form on the surface and the edges look set.
   - Flip the pancakes and cook for an additional 1-2 minutes, or until golden brown and cooked through.
7. **Repeat:**
   - Continue cooking the remaining batter in batches, greasing the griddle as needed between batches.
8. **Serve:**
   - Serve the Poi Pancakes warm with your favorite pancake toppings such as butter, maple syrup, honey, or fresh fruits.

9. **Enjoy:**
   - Enjoy the unique flavor and slight purple hue of Poi Pancakes, which offer a taste of Hawaiian tradition with a twist. Adjust the sweetness or texture by adding more sugar or buttermilk according to your preference.

These Poi Pancakes are a delightful way to incorporate the flavors of Hawaii into your breakfast or brunch. They provide a unique and nutritious twist on a classic pancake recipe, perfect for enjoying with family and friends.

Ahi Tuna Burgers

Ingredients:

- 1 lb fresh ahi tuna steaks, skin removed
- 1 tablespoon soy sauce
- 1 tablespoon sesame oil
- 1 tablespoon lime juice
- 1 teaspoon grated ginger
- 1 garlic clove, minced
- 1/4 cup panko breadcrumbs
- 1 green onion, finely chopped
- 1 tablespoon cilantro, chopped
- Salt and pepper, to taste
- 4 burger buns
- Lettuce, tomato slices, avocado slices (optional, for serving)

Instructions:

1. **Prepare the Ahi Tuna:**
   - Dice the ahi tuna steaks into small pieces and place them in a mixing bowl.
2. **Make the Marinade:**
   - In a small bowl, whisk together soy sauce, sesame oil, lime juice, grated ginger, and minced garlic.
3. **Marinate the Tuna:**
   - Pour the marinade over the diced tuna and toss to coat evenly. Let it marinate for about 15-20 minutes in the refrigerator.
4. **Prepare the Burger Patties:**
   - Remove the marinated tuna from the refrigerator. Add panko breadcrumbs, chopped green onion, chopped cilantro, salt, and pepper to the tuna mixture. Mix gently until combined.
5. **Form the Patties:**
   - Divide the tuna mixture into 4 equal portions. Shape each portion into a patty about 1-inch thick. Handle them gently to keep the patties from falling apart.
6. **Cook the Tuna Burgers:**
   - Preheat a grill or grill pan over medium-high heat. Brush the grill grates with oil to prevent sticking.
   - Grill the tuna burgers for about 3-4 minutes per side, or until they are cooked to your desired doneness. Ahi tuna is typically served rare to medium-rare for best flavor and texture.
7. **Toast the Burger Buns:**
   - While the burgers are cooking, lightly toast the burger buns on the grill or in a toaster oven until golden brown.
8. **Assemble the Burgers:**

- Place a grilled tuna burger on each toasted bun.
		- Add lettuce, tomato slices, and avocado slices if desired.
9. **Serve:**
		- Serve the Ahi Tuna Burgers immediately while warm.
		- Enjoy the fresh and flavorful tuna burgers with your favorite side dishes or a light salad.

These Ahi Tuna Burgers are a healthy and delicious alternative to beef burgers, offering a burst of seafood flavor with a hint of Asian-inspired marinade. Adjust the seasonings and toppings according to your preference for a personalized gourmet burger experience at home.

Pineapple Coconut Bars

Ingredients:

For the Crust:

- 1 1/2 cups graham cracker crumbs
- 1/2 cup unsalted butter, melted
- 1/4 cup granulated sugar

For the Pineapple Coconut Layer:

- 1 can (20 oz) crushed pineapple, drained well
- 2 cups sweetened shredded coconut
- 1 can (14 oz) sweetened condensed milk
- 1/2 cup chopped macadamia nuts (optional, for added crunch)

Instructions:

1. **Preheat the Oven:**
    - Preheat your oven to 350°F (175°C). Grease a 9x13-inch baking dish or line it with parchment paper for easy removal.
2. **Prepare the Crust:**
    - In a medium bowl, mix together the graham cracker crumbs, melted butter, and granulated sugar until well combined.
    - Press the mixture firmly into the bottom of the prepared baking dish to form an even crust.
3. **Prepare the Filling:**
    - In a large bowl, combine the drained crushed pineapple, sweetened shredded coconut, and sweetened condensed milk. Mix until thoroughly combined.
    - If using, fold in chopped macadamia nuts for added texture and flavor.
4. **Assemble and Bake:**
    - Spread the pineapple coconut mixture evenly over the prepared crust in the baking dish.
5. **Bake:**
    - Bake in the preheated oven for 25-30 minutes, or until the edges are golden brown and the center is set.
6. **Cool and Serve:**
    - Allow the Pineapple Coconut Bars to cool completely in the baking dish on a wire rack.
    - Once cooled, cut into squares or bars.
7. **Optional Garnish:**
    - Garnish with additional shredded coconut or a sprinkle of powdered sugar before serving, if desired.
8. **Enjoy:**

- Serve these Pineapple Coconut Bars as a delicious dessert or treat, perfect for tropical-themed parties or anytime you crave a taste of the islands.

These bars are sweet, chewy, and packed with tropical flavors from the pineapple and coconut. They are easy to make and sure to be a hit with friends and family alike. Adjust the sweetness by reducing the amount of sugar if you prefer a less sweet dessert.

Ginger Chicken

Ingredients:

- 1 lb boneless, skinless chicken breasts or thighs, cut into bite-sized pieces
- 2 tablespoons soy sauce
- 2 tablespoons oyster sauce
- 1 tablespoon rice vinegar
- 1 tablespoon brown sugar
- 1 tablespoon cornstarch
- 2 tablespoons vegetable oil
- 3 cloves garlic, minced
- 2 tablespoons fresh ginger, minced
- 1 bell pepper, thinly sliced
- 1 medium onion, thinly sliced
- 1 teaspoon sesame oil (optional, for extra flavor)
- Green onions, chopped (for garnish)
- Cooked rice, for serving

Instructions:

1. **Marinate the Chicken:**
   - In a bowl, combine soy sauce, oyster sauce, rice vinegar, brown sugar, and cornstarch. Mix well until the sugar and cornstarch are dissolved.
   - Add the chicken pieces to the marinade. Toss to coat evenly. Let it marinate for at least 15-20 minutes.
2. **Cook the Chicken:**
   - Heat vegetable oil in a large skillet or wok over medium-high heat.
   - Add minced garlic and minced ginger to the skillet. Stir-fry for about 1 minute until fragrant.
3. **Add Chicken and Vegetables:**
   - Add the marinated chicken to the skillet. Stir-fry for 5-6 minutes, or until the chicken is cooked through and no longer pink in the center.
4. **Incorporate Vegetables:**
   - Add sliced bell pepper and onion to the skillet. Stir-fry for an additional 2-3 minutes, or until the vegetables are tender-crisp.
5. **Finish and Serve:**
   - Drizzle sesame oil over the stir-fry for extra flavor (if using).
   - Garnish with chopped green onions.
   - Serve the Ginger Chicken hot over cooked rice.
6. **Enjoy:**
   - Enjoy the aromatic and flavorful Ginger Chicken with a side of rice, providing a satisfying meal with a perfect balance of savory and ginger-spiced flavors.

This Ginger Chicken recipe is versatile and can be customized with additional vegetables or spices according to your taste preferences. It's a delicious dish that's quick and easy to prepare, making it ideal for busy weeknights or whenever you crave a tasty stir-fry at home.

Ube (Purple Yam) Cheesecake

Ingredients:

For the Crust:

- 1 1/2 cups graham cracker crumbs
- 1/4 cup granulated sugar
- 1/2 cup unsalted butter, melted

For the Cheesecake Filling:

- 16 oz (2 blocks) cream cheese, softened
- 3/4 cup granulated sugar
- 1 cup ube halaya (ube jam or purple yam paste)
- 3 large eggs
- 1/2 cup sour cream
- 1 teaspoon vanilla extract
- Purple food coloring (optional, for a more vibrant color)

For Topping (Optional):

- Whipped cream
- Ube halaya (for drizzling)
- Fresh ube slices or purple yam chips (for garnish)

Instructions:

1. **Prepare the Crust:**
    - Preheat your oven to 325°F (160°C).
    - In a bowl, combine graham cracker crumbs, sugar, and melted butter. Mix until evenly moistened.
    - Press the mixture firmly into the bottom of a 9-inch springform pan. Use the back of a spoon or measuring cup to create an even crust layer.
    - Bake the crust in the preheated oven for 10 minutes. Remove from the oven and let it cool while preparing the filling.
2. **Prepare the Cheesecake Filling:**
    - In a large mixing bowl, beat the softened cream cheese and granulated sugar until smooth and creamy.
    - Add the ube halaya (ube jam) to the cream cheese mixture. Mix until well combined.
    - Add eggs one at a time, mixing well after each addition.
    - Mix in sour cream and vanilla extract until smooth. Add purple food coloring if desired, to achieve a deeper purple color.
3. **Assemble and Bake:**

- Pour the cheesecake filling over the cooled crust in the springform pan.
- Smooth the top with a spatula to create an even surface.

4. **Bake the Cheesecake:**
   - Place the springform pan on a baking sheet to catch any drips. Bake in the preheated oven for 45-50 minutes, or until the edges are set and the center is slightly jiggly.

5. **Cool and Chill:**
   - Turn off the oven and leave the cheesecake inside with the door slightly open for 1 hour to cool gradually.
   - Remove the cheesecake from the oven and run a knife around the edge of the pan to loosen it from the sides.
   - Let the cheesecake cool completely at room temperature, then refrigerate for at least 4 hours or overnight to chill and set.

6. **Serve:**
   - Remove the cheesecake from the springform pan and transfer it to a serving platter.
   - If desired, decorate with whipped cream, drizzle with additional ube halaya, and garnish with fresh ube slices or purple yam chips.

7. **Enjoy:**
   - Slice and serve the Ube Cheesecake chilled, savoring the creamy texture and delightful ube flavor.

This Ube Cheesecake recipe celebrates the rich purple yam flavor and is perfect for special occasions or whenever you want to impress with a unique and delicious dessert. Adjust the sweetness and color intensity according to your preferences for a personalized touch.

Huli Huli Tofu

Ingredients:

- 1 block (14-16 oz) firm tofu, drained and pressed
- 1/2 cup pineapple juice
- 1/4 cup soy sauce
- 1/4 cup ketchup
- 1/4 cup brown sugar
- 2 tablespoons rice vinegar
- 1 tablespoon sesame oil
- 1 tablespoon fresh ginger, grated
- 2 cloves garlic, minced
- 1/4 teaspoon black pepper
- Optional: 1-2 tablespoons sriracha or hot sauce (for heat)
- 1 tablespoon cornstarch mixed with 2 tablespoons water (to thicken sauce)
- Sliced green onions and sesame seeds, for garnish
- Cooked rice, for serving

Instructions:

1. **Prepare the Tofu:**
   - Cut the block of tofu into 1-inch cubes or slices. Pat dry with paper towels and press the tofu to remove excess moisture.
2. **Make the Huli Huli Sauce:**
   - In a small saucepan, combine pineapple juice, soy sauce, ketchup, brown sugar, rice vinegar, sesame oil, grated ginger, minced garlic, and black pepper. Optionally, add sriracha or hot sauce for heat.
   - Bring the sauce to a simmer over medium heat. Cook for 5-7 minutes, stirring occasionally, until slightly thickened.
3. **Cook the Tofu:**
   - Heat a large skillet or grill pan over medium-high heat. Lightly grease the skillet with oil.
   - Add the tofu pieces to the skillet in a single layer. Cook for 3-4 minutes on each side, or until golden brown and crispy.
4. **Glaze with Huli Huli Sauce:**
   - Pour half of the Huli Huli sauce over the tofu in the skillet. Toss gently to coat the tofu evenly.
   - Cook for another 2-3 minutes, allowing the tofu to absorb the flavors of the sauce.
5. **Thicken the Sauce:**
   - Stir the cornstarch-water mixture into the remaining Huli Huli sauce in the saucepan.

- Cook for 1-2 minutes, stirring constantly, until the sauce thickens to your desired consistency.
6. **Serve:**
    - Serve the Huli Huli Tofu over cooked rice.
    - Drizzle the thickened Huli Huli sauce over the tofu.
    - Garnish with sliced green onions and sesame seeds.
7. **Enjoy:**
    - Enjoy this flavorful and vegetarian-friendly Huli Huli Tofu, offering a taste of Hawaiian cuisine with its sweet and tangy sauce. It's a satisfying dish that pairs well with steamed vegetables or a fresh salad.

This recipe allows you to enjoy the essence of Huli Huli flavors while incorporating tofu as a protein alternative. Adjust the sweetness or spice level of the sauce according to your preference for a personalized dish that's sure to impress.

Kalua Pork Nachos

Ingredients:

- 1 lb Kalua pork, shredded (you can make your own or use store-bought)
- 1 bag (about 10-12 oz) tortilla chips
- 2 cups shredded mozzarella cheese
- 1 cup shredded cheddar cheese
- 1/2 cup diced pineapple (fresh or canned, drained)
- 1/2 cup diced red onion
- 1/4 cup sliced jalapeños (optional, for spice)
- 1/4 cup chopped fresh cilantro (optional, for garnish)
- Sour cream, guacamole, salsa, or additional toppings as desired

Instructions:

1. **Preheat the Oven:**
    - Preheat your oven to 375°F (190°C). Line a baking sheet with parchment paper or aluminum foil for easy cleanup.
2. **Assemble the Nachos:**
    - Arrange half of the tortilla chips in a single layer on the prepared baking sheet.
    - Sprinkle half of the shredded mozzarella and cheddar cheeses evenly over the chips.
    - Spread half of the shredded Kalua pork over the cheese layer.
    - Sprinkle half of the diced pineapple, diced red onion, and sliced jalapeños (if using) over the pork.
3. **Repeat Layers:**
    - Add another layer of tortilla chips on top of the first layer.
    - Repeat the cheese, Kalua pork, pineapple, red onion, and jalapeños for the second layer.
4. **Bake the Nachos:**
    - Place the baking sheet in the preheated oven and bake for 10-15 minutes, or until the cheese is melted and bubbly.
5. **Serve:**
    - Remove the Kalua Pork Nachos from the oven.
    - Garnish with chopped fresh cilantro, if desired.
    - Serve immediately with sour cream, guacamole, salsa, or your favorite nacho toppings on the side.
6. **Enjoy:**
    - Enjoy these delicious Kalua Pork Nachos as a hearty appetizer or main dish. The smoky flavor of the Kalua pork complements the sweetness of pineapple and the crunchiness of the nachos, creating a delightful fusion of flavors.

This recipe allows you to bring a taste of Hawaii to your next gathering or game day event with a creative twist on classic nachos. Customize the toppings and adjust the spice level according to your preference for a personalized nacho experience.

Macadamia Nut Hummus

Ingredients:

- 1 can (15 oz) chickpeas (garbanzo beans), drained and rinsed
- 1/2 cup macadamia nuts
- 1/4 cup tahini (sesame paste)
- 2 cloves garlic, minced
- Juice of 1 lemon (about 2-3 tablespoons)
- 2-4 tablespoons water, as needed
- 1/4 cup extra virgin olive oil
- 1/2 teaspoon ground cumin
- Salt and pepper, to taste
- Optional garnish: chopped macadamia nuts, drizzle of olive oil, paprika, or chopped parsley

Instructions:

1. **Prepare the Macadamia Nuts:**
    - If using raw macadamia nuts, toast them in a dry skillet over medium heat for 3-4 minutes, stirring frequently, until lightly golden and fragrant. Let them cool before using.
2. **Blend Ingredients:**
    - In a food processor, combine the chickpeas, toasted macadamia nuts, tahini, minced garlic, lemon juice, and ground cumin.
    - Pulse until the mixture becomes coarse and crumbly.
3. **Add Olive Oil and Water:**
    - With the food processor running, gradually pour in the extra virgin olive oil through the feed tube. Process until the mixture is smooth and creamy.
    - If needed, add water, 1 tablespoon at a time, until the hummus reaches your desired consistency.
4. **Season to Taste:**
    - Season the Macadamia Nut Hummus with salt and pepper to taste. Adjust the lemon juice or seasoning as desired.
5. **Serve:**
    - Transfer the hummus to a serving bowl.
    - Drizzle with a little extra virgin olive oil and sprinkle with chopped macadamia nuts, paprika, or chopped parsley for garnish.
6. **Enjoy:**
    - Serve the Macadamia Nut Hummus with pita bread, vegetable sticks, or crackers. Enjoy the creamy texture and nutty flavor of this unique hummus variation.

This Macadamia Nut Hummus recipe offers a delicious alternative to traditional hummus, showcasing the buttery richness of macadamia nuts blended with classic hummus ingredients. It's perfect for entertaining or as a tasty snack that's both nutritious and satisfying. Adjust the ingredients and seasonings according to your preference for a personalized flavor profile.